FLYING IN POST-WAR SKIES

Private & Club Aviation 1946-1980

ARTHUR W. J. G. ORD-HUME

Ostensibly a Luton Airport product, the Percival P.34 Proctor 3 G-AHGA was originally built as LZ704 and civil-registered on March 29th 1946, before being withdrawn from use at Elstree in September 1963. A hark-back to the pre-war days of the all-wood light aircraft, the Proctor series derived from the earlier Gulls, in particular the Vega Gull and these were rather better-built than the immediate post-war Miles aircraft such as the Messenger and the Gemini. As a consequence, more Proctors survived through the years than the later and lighter-built (but better-finished) Miles products from Woodley.

Stenlake Publishing Ltd

First Published in the United Kingdom, 2020
Stenlake Publishing Limited
54–58 Mill Square,
Catrine, KA5 6RD
01290 551122
www.stenlake.co.uk

ISBN 978-1-84033-869-0

Printed by Blissetts, Roslin Road, Acton, W3 8DH

This experimental two-seater, built to try out a camber-changing wing-section and full-span slotted flaps devised by aerodynamicist R T Youngman, was designed by Leslie E Baynes and built by Heston Aircraft Ltd in 1947. Known as the Youngman-Baynes High Lift, G-AMBL was built using some standard parts from the Percival Proctor. It was not, however, modified from the Percival design as some have claimed. For a start the position of the wing spars was quite different so the Proctor fuselage would have been useless. Both the width and depth of the body is quite different. The undercarriage, while using Proctor spats, was extended to provide ground clearance for the flaps and the whole aircraft was engineered about the special wing. Powered by a 250 hp Gipsy Queen 32, it made its first flight on February 5th 1948 as VT789 at the hands of test pilot Flight Lieutenant Ralph S Munday. It made a public debut at the Royal Aeronautical Society's Garden Party at White Waltham on May 6th 1951 and, its experimental days completed, was presented to the College of Aeronautics at Cranfield in 1954. The slow-flying ability of this aircraft helped the understanding of post-war slow-speed aerodynamics but the weight and complexity of the system rendered it beyond the resources of manufacturers to adapt for light aircraft.

British Library Cataloguing in Publication Data:
A catalogue record for this book is available from the British Library.

Preface

My own civilian flying coincided with the end of the Second World War and, despite being financially not particularly well-off, I managed to maintain a presence on the aviation scene which allowed me access to history in the making. Domestic circumstances that restricted my activities centred on my parents as neither my father nor my mother was in good health. They were not old – Dad died at the age of 55 and Mum was just 50 – and this impinged on my RAF service where, thanks to a sympathetic commanding officer who, as it turned out, also had sick parents, I saw out the closing days of my service at RAF Hendon. This allowed me to live at home and commute to and from work by bicycle each day. This rare privilege instilled in me the importance of always being aware of the problems of others. It has stood me in good stead ever since.

However, I had interests other than mere aeroplane-flying and these were in designing and building. It may seem unlikely and even draconian today, but at that time it was virtually illegal to attempt to build and fly your own aircraft. There simply was not any legislation to cover it and intransigence in high places is by no means a modern phenomenon. As a person building his own aeroplane, therefore, I was at variance with the law! Not that I was alone in this and there were four of us across the country attempting to fly amateur aircraft in violation of the rules and regulations of the land.

Circumstances other than my parent's health were also at work. My parents were not wealthy. Where once the family had been comfortably breeched, the war years and failing heath had taken their toll. In those pre-NHS days, one had to pay your local doctor for his services. I was also in the unhappy position of being the sole bread-winner which meant that I had to finance the on-going costs of our comfortable home on a private estate at Hatch End near Pinner. I also had to have money for those unexpected emergencies that beset every family. In short I was not particularly well off. And aviation was very much an expensive luxury!

Throughout life, feet are occasionally fallen on and it was just such an occasion that generated sufficient money to enable me to complete my studies (done with the unstinting support of the RAF Education Officer at Hendon who made sure that I had plenty of time off to attend university). I also was a founder member of the Ultra Light Aircraft Association, later the Popular Flying Association, known today as the Light Aircraft Association. This gave me a foothold in a new and otherwise unrecognised market place. My co-founders in the ULAA were almost all ex-RAF officers (some very senior and retired) and hence much older than I. But all was well because they sought a level of social status – and I went along with them. We affiliated with the Royal Aero Club and consequently were allowed to make use of the Club facilities in London's prestigious Park Lane. This became our 'registered office' which looked very good on letterheads.

Meanwhile I was working at Handley-Page Ltd at Cricklewood where, as a junior draughtsman and enthusiast I was allowed to design small and unimportant things. My time there was an eye-opener to the world of aircraft design and I learned a useful maxim: don't design anything that you couldn't make yourself! After I had observed a particularly nasty example of poor evolution which turned out to be a very expensive mistake for my employers, I found myself that much the wiser. The problems arose from a row of nuts inside a closed-off wing component which turned out to be totally inaccessible by any fitter, be he massively experienced or crossed on his mother's side with a nimble mouse.

And so I learned the corollary to that earlier saying, namely don't expect anybody to *make* something that you couldn't make easily by yourself! This was something a very senior designer well above me had missed out on – and it cost our employers dearly!

Old man Handley Page was a rather eccentric fellow in his old age. His eccentricity ultimately cost him ownership of his once-great pioneering company, but that is another story. I happened to meet up with him by chance at a dinner at the Royal Aero Club where, not surprisingly, he didn't recognise me, let alone realise that he was my boss! I asked, in a matter-of-fact way, if his company had any affiliation with a flying club by which employees could fly at subsidised rates. He said no but gave me the impression that he had not thought about it and might now do so.

While he never found out who had suggested it, within weeks the company had formed the Handley Page Flying Club affiliated to Elstree Flying Club. This tie-up allowed HP Club members to fly the Elstree Club's Auster Autocrats at a greatly reduced hourly rate. The deal also included the service of flying instructors so we could also learn to fly cheaply.

From very small beginnings, I was now part of what would soon be a mechanism that drove ministerial thinking and eventually would allow both amateur aircraft building again (it was fairly prolific in the 1930s) and, even, the design of new aircraft by amateurs.

The re-introduction of the Permit to Fly system was the first major step: this allowed aircraft to operate, within accepted restrictions, without having a

Certificate of Airworthiness. The C of A applied to factory-built aircraft where every single piece of the aircraft could be checked against documentation in a paperwork chain that was not just daunting but quite out of the question as far as the amateur was concerned.

The Permit to Fly system initially applied to small, low-powered single-seat aircraft. Its systematic extension to cover almost any aircraft is a comparatively recent development and now there are home-built aircraft of all sizes, shapes and types.

The Light Aircraft Association of today has earned the respect and acceptance of the aviation industry as the expert body to supervise the airworthiness of most light aircraft. Even types which originally operated on a full (and expensive) annual C of A are now permitted to apply for operation under the Permit system.

The post-war revival of British light aircraft was thus the dawn of a wholly new aviation era. On the one hand it has seen an enormous increase in the rules and regulations that govern flying a light plane while on the other it has opened up the whole rich opportunities for amateur aircraft design and construction.

Which leads me to a rather unfortunate personal tale. The development of the British post-war light aircraft was the subject of a major two-volume book that I produced a few years ago for a foreign publishing house. It is a popular misconception that if somebody writes a book they must be wealthy. This is very far from the truth and, to be frank, one is lucky if one gets one's cash expenditure back, let alone the wherewithal for the luxury house, yacht and private jet. Anyway, after four years of hard work I produced these two books for this publisher, the edition was printed and review copies went out. The books earned a universally encouraging reception including 'Book of the Month' status with the aviation magazines. I even received a Royal Aero Club award for 'contributions to light aviation'.

It was at this point that the publisher decided to abandon publishing leaving me without a penny! The print-run was liquidated which meant that it was sold off cheap into the book trade and I got zilch! Lesson One: Never take things for granted! I was going to add 'beware smiling strangers bearing promises' but I thought that might be a bit too strong…

Which brings me nicely to this present book which is a pictorial look at the private aircraft and club flying scene from 1946. It was on January 1st that year that civil light aviation was permitted to restart after the exigencies of war. Not that it was all that simple. Being allowed to fly again was one thing. Actually having something to fly and then flying it was quite another. It was also a time when it seemed that paperwork was more important to the authorities than airworthiness.

Finally I want to explain the meaning behind the cover picture of this book. It is actually the front cover of the weekly magazine *Flight* dated August 22nd 1946, and was originally an advertisement for the Auster Autocrat which was promoted as 'The Steel Aeroplane' at a time when, in Britain, we were still in an age of wood for light aircraft. But this advert is crammed with symbolism which I accept means nothing to today's casual observer who did not live through the Second World War. Let me take you back to 1946 and give you the informed eyes with which to understand this apparently carefree and colourful, gay scene. Remember that, although the war was over, we still had food rationing and a National Debt of such size that we were totally dependent on other nations, predominantly America, to lend us cash with which to survive.

Throughout the war years, people were prohibited from going near the seaside unless they had a valid excuse and a permit. All the south and east coasts were heavily defended with mile upon mile of steel and concrete anti-invasion defences blocking every sandy beach along the south coast and the east coast all the way as far as Scotland. Almost every seaside pier had been cut in half, a central section blown up to prevent its possible use by invaders. Sailing was prohibited, so the thought of taking to the water in a small boat was quite out of the question. There were, of course, no seaside hotels or boarding-houses and the beach was a 'no-go' area patrolled by armed troops.

To think of a free seaside where one could visit a sandy shore, stroll along a pier and sip cool drinks under a gaily-coloured umbrella was thus but a distant memory for the elders and an unknown experience for the youngsters. As for flying a light aircraft over the coast, this, too, was unthinkable. This simple and colourful piece of artwork is therefore filled with allegory and was deeply emblematic of those better times for which we cried out for.

The dual control Auster Autocrat with its two front seats and its curious sideways-placed 'secretary'-seat in the back may have been the Leicestershire-built British version of an American light plane design created by a frustrated English designer working Stateside, but it came to be a mainstay for the rather bleak post-war club and private-owner scene.

Those first decades after the Second World War were an uphill struggle which on the one hand were refreshingly free from too much legislative control when actually flying while on the other hands were tied as to what we could, couldn't and mustn't do. Few were the 'restricted areas' and right up into the 1960s, you could fly happily without radio over the top of Heathrow so long as you were above 4,000 feet, or you could fly round it so long as you kept three miles from the end of its runway. This meant that you flew over the old airfield at Langley. The civil servants had yet to conjure up their lists of restrictions.

Overall, though, flying an aeroplane was seen rather as a privilege, not a right!

Wanted! Aeroplanes

The 1939-45 war took its toll on the light aviation movement in the British Isles. This was not just a single, definable entity, but a widespread and extended effect that impinged on every aspect of life. Over and above all the exigencies of continued food shortage, rationing and a sustained fuel crisis was the towering spectre of the National Debt. We may have won the war but it had cost us dearly. A pyrrhic victory in virtually every aspect! As a nation we were simply broke with no money and precious few prospects.

To make matters worse, we suffered a terrible winter with weather conditions that paralysed the transport system for many months. The result of this was that power stations could not be supplied with coal and coal was needed to generate electricity. Not only had we no public transport, but we had grossly restricted domestic power. Even the factories had to shut down.

It wasn't a healthy situation, even for a country that could pay its way. For one that had no reserves of anything including cash, it was nothing short of a disaster. We had to go cap-in-hand to the Americans and urge them to grub-stake Britain and its people, in other words, beg for money to tide us over. Thank goodness we had the Americans for, whatever may have happened since, the close ties between London and Washington paid off and the Yanks agreed to lend us a huge sum of cash reserves. Make no mistake: without the help we received from across the Atlantic we would probably not have survived, certainly not economically.

Small wonder, in an environment like this, something like private and sporting flying was rather low on the agenda! When the chips are down, there's only one thing on the mind – survival.

Of course, there was business. People did try to get on with their lives as best they could, and the entrepreneurial spirit was certainly not crushed. It was just that there was a highly-restricted window of opportunity. For some, there was less of a struggle than for others: that's the inevitable way of things. In the same way that some people made a fortune out of the Wall Street Crash of 1929, our economy may have been dire for the masses, but for a select few who could benefit from cheap and abundant labour and landlords who were so poor that they were open to any offer to bring in cash, these were times of opportunity.

Aviation, aircraft and flying had undergone a massive change as a result of five years of war. And it was not just in hardware, aids, techniques and skills

By far the oldest aircraft to remain airworthy and active well into the 21st century was the DH.53 Humming Bird, G-EBHZ. First flown on October 2nd 1923, it took part in the 1923 *Daily Mail* Light Aeroplane Competition at Lympne which was staged to try and find a suitable design for a single seat British aircraft. While many of the other entrants were no more than gliders to which an engine had been fitted, the DH.53 was a practical strut-braced, low wing monoplane, albeit fitted with a low power 750 cc Douglas motorcycle engine. While the Humming Bird won no prizes, it demonstrated fuel economy and strength by performing aerobatics. The aircraft entered limited production and the RAF took some: these were powered by the 698 cc 26 hp Blackburn Tomtit twin cylinder inverted V engine. G-EBHX survived into modern times and was a popular flying exhibit at the Shuttleworth Collection, Old Warden. However this all ended on July 1st 2012, when the aircraft unexpectedly and for no obvious reason dived vertically into the ground during a demonstration. Although the airframe was not badly damaged, pilot Trevor Roche was killed instantly.

but also in admin and, while admin is about as exciting to most as a bunch of dead flowers, the admin here affected us all and did not just put the brakes on 'grass-roots' aviation but it killed it off.

Before the war, all types of aircraft certification came under the jurisdiction of just one authority – the Air Ministry. The Air Ministry was responsible for flying clubs and Authorisations to Fly for home-built aircraft, as well as for ordering front-line supercharged biplane fighters for the Royal Air Force.

There was no distinction between military and civilian aircraft and in the 1930s this didn't matter much. During the war years and immediately afterwards, the Air Ministry recognised that the gap between civil and military aircraft was expanding and becoming a chasm as performance, operation and development standards became ever more divergent. So was formed the Ministry of Civil Aviation and with it the Air Registration Board to cater for the increasing responsibilities of design and construction standards.

This was an obvious development progression as it catered for the changing needs of commercial aircraft operation and development and the very different and more flexible needs of service aviation. And private aircraft naturally fell in at the bottom of the ambit of the Ministry of Civil Aviation.

There was one casualty of this legislative restructuring and that was amateur aviation which embraced home-built aircraft and those machines which, in pre-war years, had operated outside the auspices of formal Air Ministry-governed civilian aviation with its Certificates of Airworthiness. This was the small group of machines that flew under a Permit to Fly.

Suddenly it was found that these aircraft had slipped through the net of the new system and been left stateless. Machines such as BAC Drones, the single-seat Tipsy S.2 and Dart Kitten, all home-builts such as Luton Minors, Perman Parasols and others were now in limbo, existing in a paperwork void from which escape seemed impossible.

A flurry of letters from frustrated flyers who had carefully preserved their cherished aircraft all through the war years in the fervent hope of renewing flying days once peace was re-established spattered the correspondence pages of the aviation press. Relatively speaking, there were not too many of them and the authorities thought that if they ignored them they might simply give up and go away. They didn't though, and eventually the Ministry of Aviation relented and gave these people until December 31st 1948, to apply for a Permit to Fly. To apply and be granted that cherished Permit, however, the applicant had to have an airworthy machine which had been signed off by a competent engineer as structurally sound and airworthy (i.e. test-flown) complete with insurance and a qualified pilot.

Not all the people who wanted to apply could meet all those obligations. Many, wisely, had not chosen to invest in completing a part-built aircraft until the certainty of subsequent Permit status was guaranteed and the time left was too short for the time

One would be hard-pushed to describe the Desoutter as an attractive aircraft. Unlike the similar-sized Leopard and Puss Moths from Stag Lane, the Desoutter was angular, ugly and cramped to get in and out of. But it flew surprisingly well and was popular with those who didn't object to its appearance or its non-responsive ailerons. In fact it was the ailerons which gave the most trouble with at least three different types of hinge system being tried. G-AAPZ is a veteran from August 1931 and was first owned by National Flying Services Ltd which had the idea of using the type as a sort of 'universal trainer'. It didn't happen. This aircraft was the owned by Richard Ormonde Shuttleworth (1909-1940). He was in the RAF and lost his life in a Fairey Battle. Today this aircraft is preserved at the Shuttleworth Trust, Old Warden. It was flown regularly until 2010 when aileron flutter alarmed its demonstration pilot since which time it has been grounded.

and cash investment to complete. Home-made aircraft were in the hobby class and could not be built in weeks, but more like years And others could not insure and test-fly an aircraft that was without a Permit… it was so often a case of 'heads you win and tails I lose'.

Three particular constructors stand out from this time – A C Waterhouse of Clifton, Rugby, and his BAC Drone G-ADPJ, D E 'Ted' Felce of Hinckley, Leicestershire, and his Luton Minor, later registered as G-ALUZ, and Robert Henry 'Bob' Parker of Hinchley Wood, Esher, Surrey, with his Heath Parasol G-AFZE. These men were at the forefront of the growing conflict with the authorities. I had my own problems over G-AFIR, so I was a fourth sufferer.

Waterhouse had the worst luck of all: as soon as he got close to being able to apply for a Permit, something happened to set him back to square-one (on one occasion a gale blew a hangar door onto his aircraft and literally flattened it). Felce had endless problems with his Scott Flying Squirrel engine and trying to make a usable propeller for it. And Parker's tiny Blackburne Tomtit engine would barely get his aircraft into the air, a circuit being, as it turned out, a mammoth undertaking.

The amateur end of flying was, as the 1940s came to a close, up against a brick wall. The light aircraft movement, though, was free to flourish – provided it could find something to flourish with.

In the 1930s, Britain was predominant in light aircraft construction and, to a large extent, 'ruled the world' in light and club aircraft design and construction as well as sales. All these aircraft, however, were predominantly made of wood. Admittedly the DH.82a Tiger Moth had a steel tubular fuselage, but the remainder of it was of timber.

Changes, though, were afoot in particular in America where, by 1936, tubular steel structures that were welded rather than bolted together were becoming the norm. By 1939, while we were still selling Moths, Hawks and Gulls in America, many of the up-coming American aircraft under development had tubular steel primary structure. Some even had all-metal monocoque structures that were close-riveted.

When war broke out in 1939, our light aircraft industry virtually ceased overnight. This did not happen in America where, apart from an increasing difficulty in obtaining materials later in the war, light aircraft design, development and construction continued unabated. In any case, America was not at war with anybody – yet. The upshot was that in 1946 we were left with a diminished stock of pre-war aircraft plus the awakening of those lucky enough to have survived Impressment. Meanwhile, thanks to less stringent wartime manufacturing restrictions, America was offering the world new types and designs.

Avro Sport Avian G-ABEE was owned by a group of vintage aircraft enthusiasts at Denham in the late forties. A true 'old-timer' of the skies, this delightful aircraft with its ADC Cirrus Hermes engine was a true joy to fly and was in strong demand by those who were privileged to fly it. Its ultimate demise was quite unforgiveable. In 1954 the original Vintage Group folded as members died or moved on. With hangarage both restricted and expensive at Denham, G-ABEE was flown to White Waltham where we were told it could be parked for a while free of charge in an open blister hangar. In May of 1955, a group of Popular Flying Association enthusiasts got together and formed plans for a full restoration of the aircraft. All went well until the Whit Monday air display at White Waltham where the author witnessed a swarm, of 'aircraft enthusiasts', young and not so young, who descended on the Avian in its open hangar and systematically stripped it of everything of value. Instruments were removed, fabric was even cut from the fuselage. Intervention from the police did not deter these alleged spotters. By the end of the day, G-ABEE was beyond economic repair. The story was related in *Air Pictorial* that July.

Although at first sight somewhat similar, the two Leeds-built metal-framed aerobatic Arrow Active biplanes differed in a number of significant ways. The Mk.I, G-ABIX, was powered by a 115 hp Cirrus Hermes IIB and had a Comper Swift type centre-section upper wing pylon that was built integrally with the fuselage to support the top wing, and a small fin. The fabric on the rear fuselage was laced like that of many First World War aircraft. The designer was Arthur Cecil Thornton, who had earlier been responsible for the Blackburn Bluebird. This Active was destroyed when, on December 30th 1935, racing pilot Alex Henshaw suffered an in-flight engine fire while practising aerobatics. Fortunately he was able to escape by parachute but the Arrow was lost crashing at Marshfield, East Lindsay, 11 miles SE of Grimsby. The Mk.II Active stands behind in this picture. This was powered by a 120 hp DH Gipsy III and had a strut-braced centre-section and a small header fuel tank above the centre-section. A much longer cockpit fairing almost extended to the fin leading edge. This Active survived to fly extensively after the war.

Besides losing our role as the makers of the world's light aircraft, we were thoroughly out-gunned. The battle was lost, however, begrudgingly and there was at first a strong resistance to buying American light aircraft. Apart from the fundamental fact that we didn't have the currency to spend on such luxuries, there was an overriding objection to US light planes best described by the commonest of all objections – 'they've all got funny screw-threads'. True it was that the time-honoured Aircraft & General Stores (AGS) parts classification was useless when it came to attempting to service a US-built aircraft, but the fact that it was probably slightly better-built was largely overlooked.

Gradually, however, such prejudices were forgotten and the sheer utility of the Yankee light planes won over the day. There was still the matter of currency, though, and while distributors were appointed in the UK for the popular American types such as Piper and Cessna, not everybody could access those precious foreign funds.

By 1930 there was a major obstacle to importing light aircraft from abroad, especially America and this was the imposition of a 30 percent import tax. While several wealthy private owners were unfazed by this, mass ownership of what some saw as desirable light planes made outside the UK, was severely hampered by this high rate of duty. Two companies sought to avoid this by forming a separate UK manufacturing arm. One was Taylorcraft Aeroplanes which later became Auster, and the other was Aeronca, the Aeronautical Corporation of Great Britain acting as a British maker of the original US Aeronca C.3. One of these succeeded while the other failed. The economy of flying two people on 37 horsepower from two cylinders was considered as rather pushing it a bit. Even the Czechoslovakian Praga E.114, designed by Jaroslav ·lechta and first flown in 1934, had 40 hp from four cylinders at its disposal.

This matter of relative size came to a head in the 1930s. By the end of the 1920s it was reported in the aviation press that amateur aircraft construction was now all-but banned and home-made aircraft were to all intents and purposes illegal. It wasn't that there was a classification for home-builts against which somebody had written 'Restricted', it was more a case of there being no classification for the genre. And in an age when paperwork was God, no classification meant that it didn't and couldn't exist.

Matters came to an unexpected head when the

Frenchman Henri Mignet invented his Pou-du-Ciel or, as we British called it, the Flying Flea. Suddenly people started building these tiny aeroplanes in the very real expectation that they would be allowed to fly them when they were complete. The Air Ministry had to think fast and, fearing a mass rebellion if it stood its ground, quickly thought up legislation to allow these non-C of A aircraft to fly. It was called the Permit to Fly. In truth it was an extension of an existing scheme whereby an aircraft which for some reason or another did not have a valid C of A. The then-existing Permit scheme allowed an aircraft to be permitted a positioning flight for, for example, overhaul or modification.

The new revised category of Permit to Fly applied to aircraft that were not factory-built but made in garages, bedrooms and back gardens by amateurs.

As far as Britain was concerned, the Mignet design was not alone in availing itself of the P to F scheme for, inspired by Henri Mignet's sheer hotspur, other would-be flyers started designing and building their own aircraft. Some were successful, others were not but, over and above all this was the comforting knowledge that when you built your aircraft, there was the Permit to Fly system which would allow you to fly it legally. Those who depended on this pre-war arrangement, however, were in for a post-war shock.

In the 1930s, the difference in size and performance of top-line RAF aircraft and the top end of private aircraft was not all that great and the Air Ministry, traditionally involved in the official side of looking after all things that flew, were able to have no outward qualms about dealing with Hawker Fury fighter-bomber one moment and flying clubs with Miles Hawks the next. By the end of the war, however, the gap between private and Service aircraft, not to mention those in commercial operation, was vastly greater. Private and club aircraft in Britain were still usually made of wood with fabric covering. Fighter aircraft were now immensely more powerful, all metal creations with advanced attributes in the way of supercharged engines, flaps and slots, hydraulics, pneumatics and electrics. And jet engines were on the horizon. It was a long leap between the club Tiger Moth and the Typhoon or Lancaster. Civil aviation needed a separate legislative and the problem was not just Britain but world wide.

The outcome of this was the holding of an international meeting in Chicago, USA. This was the Convention on International Civil Aviation, widely known as the Chicago Convention, which took place while war still raged. Its aims and objects, originally published in 1944, stated that signatories should collectively work to harmonize and standardize the use of airspace for safety, efficiency and regularity of air transport.

Each signatory country, of which there are now at least 188, had to establish a civil aviation authority to oversee the various forms of operation specific to areas of civil aviation. The document was signed on December 7th 1944, initially by 52 signatory states. It took effect on April 4th 1947, and, in Britain, was the mandate of the newly-formed Ministry of Civil Aviation.

As far as we in Britain were concerned, this created a body that looked after private and club aircraft on the one hand, and airliners and charter aeroplanes on the other. Somewhere down the line, a whole sector of the civil aircraft market had fallen out of the regime which had been the realm of the Air Ministry and was now lost in the creation of the new Government Ministry. That sector was amateur aviation as demonstrated by home-built aircraft and aircraft that did not qualify for the full Certificate of Airworthiness.

It was a battle of paperwork to reinstate the Permit scheme and expand it to allow newly-built aircraft and new designs to be included. The home-built aeroplane movement triumphed – but it was an uphill struggle. We got there in the end, though.

Back to the immediate post-war years, the future was unclear and seemed a long way ahead. We had stayed still in amateur flying while the rest of the world, it seemed, had moved on. Certainly the Americans had, and the transatlantic light plane was now a sophisticated piece of kit. Cessna advertised its latest tin plane which had a tricycle undercarriage and what it promoted as 'Land-o-Matic Flaps' by the use of which landing, it implied, was a doddle.

In later years, several well-documented tales emanated from the land of Uncle Sam where quite young children had successfully landed a light plane following the incapacitation of the pilot merely by reading the instruments and remembering what they had seen the pilot do with the control wheel. In one instance, a small boy had the misfortune to be in the air when his father, the pilot, suffered a heart attack and died. The boy had the confidence to make a successful return to earth. Much of this was down to the refinement of the aircraft and its systems as well as the undoubted courage of the young pilot in charge.

We had new aeroplanes. They came from Rearsby and were bright and fresh. What we didn't at once know was that many of these were re-manufactured from military Taylorcraft Austers. Not that it mattered much, but deep down it confirmed that Britain had lost five, getting on for six years, of progress and development. Our smart Miles Magisters were also mainly tarted-up government surplus. The new British light aircraft was something of an oxymoron.

Now this was not a bad thing because what was available was cheap and newly-manufactured aircraft like the idiosyncratic Chrislea Ace and the delightful Newbury EoN were realistically priced – and this meant that they were priced out of most people's pockets. The flying clubs were the main customers for aircraft and it made much more sense to buy six Tiger Moths for £50 each (or less) and give them a comprehensive rebuild and probably still come in under the cost of one new aircraft.

When British civil flying enthusiasts were allowed to get back into skies that were now peaceful again, they had a raggle-tag bunch of ancient pre-war aircraft, war planes that had been released for private flying, and a choice of very few new aircraft. The new aircraft were pricey. We were prevented from buying from overseas. It wasn't a particularly encouraging picture. It was an age of austerity dominated by paperwork and without the proper paperwork you could not fly. Over and above all that there was a government urge to bring in foreign currency at all costs. And there were parts of the world where money was not circumscribed and British light aircraft were still attractive. Aircraft brokers thus saw it their job to sell whatever old British aircraft they could lay their hands on in return for good money.

And so it was that every week our aviation weekly magazines – *Flight* and *The Aeroplane* – were filled with ads for pre-war Miles Speed Sixes, de Havilland Moths, and just about everything else you could think of. What we didn't get airborne in ourselves risked being sold abroad.

No wonder we began to eye the French and certainly the Americans with envy. Great Britain was, as far as club and private aircraft were concerned, Poor Britain. That we survived all this was something of a miracle. And it was not due to a thriving British industry – that died a painful death with Beagle in the 1967 – but due to small business and, above all, amateur aviation and home-building.

Britain's aircraft industry moved from the factory to the private garage, living room and back garden!

In this little book I hope to be able to remind you of the struggle that began in 1946 and developed into the true freedom of the air (albeit with infinitely increased operational restrictions) that we have today. My photographs, as ever, have come from many sources and are chosen for what they portray and their rarity. And as usual the quality is variable. Only the message is unspoiled.

The surviving Arrow Active Mk.II was systematically modified over the years after the war and the original fin, clearly a legacy of the old Bluebird, was reshaped and faired into the cockpit fairing. Dunlop wheels and tyres replaced the original 1920s-style ones. This was first flown in June of 1932 and was test-flown by Arthur Geoffrey Wincott. A King's Cup competitor in both 1932 and 1933, it was stored at Yeadon until 1957 when it was restored for Norman Jones and the Tiger Club. At the same time it was re-engined with a 145 hp Gipsy Major IC. Spanning just 24 feet, the Active had a top speed of 144 mph and is still in existence.

The sole Arrow Active 2 from 1932 still survives into the 21st century to remind us of the days when biplanes proliferated. As recently as 2016 this machine was offered for sale at just under €100,000.

The DH.80A Puss Moth was a rare survivor of pre-war years, but a number did come through the war years unscathed. One was this example, G-ABLS, first registered in May of 1931 and initially owned by Eric Gander-Dower, the well-known airline pioneer in Scotland. It participated in the 1933 and 1934 King's Cup Races at the hands of racing pilot Richard Seeley before being passed to the Aberdeen Flying School. Stored from 1939 to 1945 at Dyce, it was dug out of its enforced retirement and restored at Southampton by Cliff C Lovell after which it passed into the hands of Shuttleworth Collection pilot Captain Roger C F Bailey. In its handsome highly polished black and gold livery, it was photographed here on June 26th 1978.

The Civilian Coupé was built by the Civilian Aircraft Co Ltd of Burton-on-Trent. The work of veteran designer Harold D Boultbee formerly of Handley Page, the wooden two-seat Coupé was the company's only design. The engine in the prototype was the 75 hp ABC Hornet flat four but production machines – there were five more after the first – had the 100 hp Genet Major I radial and were styled the Mk.II. Only one survived the turbulent 'thirties and that was this one, G-ABNT painted light and dark blue. Stored carefully in a garage by G O Ross of Cardiff, it was restored and flew again in the 1990s.

The Robinson Redwing first saw the light of day in 1930. A side-by-side two-seater with an 80 hp Armstrong-Siddeley Genet IIA radial engine, it was a popular aircraft but suffered from a design fault – the undercarriage attachment at the top longeron, which also took one of the engine-mounting attachments, was prone to breakage in a heavy landing. It was this weakness that quickly eroded the dozen examples built. In 1944 there was a derelict hangar at Elstree packed with surplus government office furniture. The order was that the building was to be cleared and everything burned. While scrounging to see if there was anything useful to be liberated, the author found parts of an old aircraft scattered throughout the condemned contents. These turned out to be the dismantled components of G-ABNX, the ninth aircraft built by Redwing Aircraft at Croydon and first flown on July 2nd 1931. In a superhuman effort with two friends, the bits were separated from the old desks and chairs and the complete aircraft 'stolen' to be stored in the hangar of the Experimental Group, ULAA. Miraculously, logbooks and vital paperwork were found in the cockpit. When the Group moved to Redhill prior to demolition of its hangar preparatory to construction of the new reservoir, the Redwing went with them by road and was subsequently overhauled by the College of Aeronautical Engineering. In 1959 John Pothecary and Ted Gould restored engine and airframe and brought G-ABNX back to the skies for an illustrious new lease of life.

Pictured over Sandown Airport on August 8th 1965, is a typical formation of the time, every one of them dating from pre-war days. The Robinson Redwing G-ABNX rescued from a premature end at Elstree is being flown by John Pothecary. Spartan Arrow G-ABWP was another survivor of the turbulent times and flew for post-war years giving pleasure to many, among them John Edwards who flew her here. G-AAWO was a de Havilland DH.60G Moth which first saw the light of day in May of 1930. This Stag Lane veteran is seen here in the hands of John Reid. The sound of the Gipsy engine, the Hermes and the Genet Major radial was one to be relished!

After the end of the war, a surprising number of small aircraft, hidden away during the years of conflict, came to light and one of these was the famous racing single-seat Comper Swift, G-ABUS with its Pobjoy radial engine. Resident for a while in the hangar of the Experimental Group of the Ultra Light Aircraft Association at Elstree in Hertfordshire, this became the property of de Havilland Technical College student Tony Cole of near-by Hatfield who became one of the leading lights of that small racing fraternity which promoted itself during the 1950s as 'The Throttle-Benders Club'. The Swift was painted black and white and was later owned by David Ogilvy who was chief flying instructor of Elstree Flying Club.

Besides the rather non-standard low-powered prototype, some 41 standard Pobjoy-powered Comper Swifts were built in 1931-32 plus three special high-powered ones with in-line Gipsy engines. These were made in small batches and the first of the 1932 production was G-ABTC. This passed into the hands of RCAF officer John F Reed at Cricklade in 1939 and he stored it during the war in Wiltshire. At the end of the war this was found and presented to the Experimental Group of the Ultra Light Aircraft Association at Elstree. It was planned to restore it, but the aircraft paperwork was incomplete – at that time a 'kiss of death' for any flying machine – and the Group did not have sufficient funds to pursue their mandate adequately. After several years of storage and inevitable further deterioration it was passed into the enthusiastic hands of John Alexander Kent (1914-85), a Canadian-born pilot rated as 'one of the best young squadron leaders of the war'. Unfortunately, G-ABTC was taken by road from Elstree and was involved in an accident with a lamp-standard on the way through London. This necessitated a major rebuild but G-ABTC did fly again. Here it is at Biggin Hill on May 18th 1974.

The Hermes II-powered Spartan Arrow G-ABWP first saw the light of day in 1932, being registered on May 18th that year. The one-time property of Richard Ormonde Shuttleworth (1909–40), it saw out the war years in storage at Old Warden and was eventually restored to the Spartan Group at Denham. The venerable old biplane was a regular flyer right up into the 1970s when it went into storage. One day perhaps we will see it in the air again – a grand relic of the days of folding-wing biplanes with open cockpits.

The Avro Tutor series goes right back to 1930 and G-ACHP was a variant known as the Avro 638 Club Cadet which replaced the usual Genet Major radial with the in-line DH Gipsy Major I, the five-drop in horsepower no doubt being compensated by the reduction in aerodynamic drag from seven eager radial cylinders. Besides an improvement in overall performance, the Gipsy's smaller frontal area also improved fuel consumption. This handsome unstaggered biplane was used during the war as Saunders-Roe's communications aircraft based at Somerton on the Isle of Wight but in the post-war years it was the cherished mount of the Denham-based Vintage Aircraft Club. On January 1st 1956, determined to start the New Year with a bang, Handley Page flight test observer 'Jock' Ogilvie climbed aboard G-ACHP and took off right into the path of a line-squall. The venerable Cadet was struck by a gust and stalled. It crashed into the trees off Denham's smooth grass and was wrecked beyond repair. Jock was unhurt…

A stalwart from the olden days was G-ADHE, a de Havilland DH.60GIII Moth Major. The very last survivor of its breed, it was resident at Denham for many years in the decades that followed the war. A delight to fly, this straight-winged, staggerless Moth was comfortable and easy to handle and had a useful record of pre-war race successes to its name. Gipsy Major-powered and one of only 27 made for the British Register, G-ADHE was a breath of fresh air from the colourful skies of the past. In many ways it was nicer to fly than the Tiger Moth it spawned. The long under-fuselage exhaust pipe meant it was quieter in the air. While in the care of V B 'Dickie' Nightscale at the little Buckinghamshire airfield started in the early 1930s by a Harley Street surgeon, John Miles Bickerton, and the famous circus proprietor, Bertram Mills (with his Hornet Moth, G-ADMS), the veteran Moth was flown by Cyril Mills. He was the son of the circus founder, Cyril Bertram Mills (1902-91), and had flown a Hornet Moth in the thirties before embarking on a most distinguished wartime career in the field of espionage. Post-war he was co-owner of the circus (which always opened at Olympia in London) along with his brother. On March 22nd 1958, G-ADHE once named *Hop Along*, crashed and a famed type was extinguished – until very recently when several examples were brought back from ancient export. My picture was taken at Shoreham on September 11th 1949.

In the decades following the war, DH.60GIII Moth Major was the last of its type. It was kept in flying order at Denham and operated by the Vintage Aeroplane Club, a group of pilots who venerated the open cockpit days and relished the delights of the wind singing in the bracing-wires. Owned by Percy Eric Hindmarsh, many people flew the aircraft at Denham in the 1950s. Ownership passed to Victor Beresford Nightingale, the resident engineer, who made sure it was always available to those who wanted to fly it. On March 22nd 1958, engine failure brought a terminal crash at Shepherd Lane, Mill End, Rickmansworth.

Not all aircraft have 60th birthday parties but party-time it was at Oaksey in Wiltshire in June 1996 when Bernard Harding chose to celebrate the long life of his de Havilland Hornet Moth, G-ADNE which was named *Ariadne*. While Greek mythology would have Ariadne, daughter of Pasiphae and the Cretan king Minos, help her lover put paid to the Minataur and then escape the Labyrinth with the aid of a ball of wool, this 1936-registered DH.87B had an almost equally chequered life. It was impressed as X9325, flew throughout the war, survived several minor crashes, served, among others, Armstrong Whitworth Aircraft as a communications hack – and came through it all to be beautifully restored. Painted red and silver outlined in black, despite several subsequent minor mishaps, *Ariadne* still flies.

Owned and operated by Cartwright Hamilton Aviation, this Miles M.7W Hawk Trainer, G-ADWT, was first registered on November 6th 1935 and was impressed during the war serving as NF750. Restored on September 9th 1946, it was a regular flyer in post-war skies until 1964 when it was sold to Canada as CF-NXT. This registration was cancelled in November 1984.

Another pre-war type to survive into post-war skies was the BAC Drone powered glider which was originally designed in the early 1930s by Charles H Lowe-Wylde. First registered in August of 1935, G-ADPJ, pictured here, had a most chequered life in the 1950s and 1960s. Owned by A C Waterhouse, it was initially prohibited from flying due to the intransigence of the government over re-starting the pre-war Permit to Fly system. Waterhouse, though, persevered and his Drone did indeed fly again only to suffer a most horrendous mishap when a heavy steel hangar door, dislodged by a gale, flattened it in its hangar. Dogged determination saw it rebuilt and flown again by its owner.

Several BAC Drones survived the war including this one, John Fricker's G-AEKV with a Carden-Ford engine mounted as a pusher above the wing centre-section. A powered single-seat variant of a Gravesend-built two-seat tandem glider, the Drone was developed from the Lowe-Wylde Planette. After the designer's untimely death (it is thought he suffered a mid-air heart-attack and died while on a demo flight), production was moved to Hanworth under the control of Robert Kronfeld. Here the pusher engine – a 30 hp Carden-Ford water-cooled modified car engine) is receiving some attention. This particular aircraft is now resident at Brooklands Museum in Surrey.

The Blackburn B.2 was an all-metal side-by-side two-seat trainer first seen at the SBAC Show at Hendon on June 27th 1932. A popular aircraft, it was widely used by Flying Training Ltd at Hanworth in the years before the war. Unfortunately, many met premature ends through fire or crash with the result that when private flying started up in 1946, just two examples remained – G-ACLD and this one, G-AEBJ. The former was being demonstrated at York when it crashed on June 16th 1951, through stalling off a turn. Faith in slots was not inviolate! The sole survivor, G-AEBJ, was restored by its makers at Brough and flown at important events. In this picture, besides showing off the B.2's slots, there's a special Gloster Meteor two-seater in the background. A PV7-8, G-ANSO was a hybrid created by fitting a Mk.7 two-seat cockpit to the decommissioned ground attack prototype, G-7-1. This was first flown in August 1951 and went to Bromma, Sweden, in 1959. The B.2 still flies.

Developed from the 1927 German Klemm L.25, the BA Swallow was an English-designed version which, while maintaining the superb flying characteristics of the original, was rather more modern (by 1930s standard) in appearance. While structurally similar to its original, the new model was manufactured at Hanworth by British Klemm Aeroplane Company Ltd, later to change its name to British Aircraft Company. Works manager was George H Handasyde – the 'Martinsyde' man – and test pilot was E G Horton. One can imagine that the BA re-design of the L.25 was mainly Handasyde's work. Three versions were made. First was the BK.1 Swallow fitted with either the 85 hp Pobjoy R or the 75 hp Salmson AD.9 engines of which 28 were built. Next was the BA. 2 Swallow which was 90 hp Pobjoy Cataract-powered and resulted in a 59-strong production run. Third was the 90 hp Cirrus-powered variant of the BA.2 of which 47 were made. One example of all the Swallows made was converted to the Swallow Coupé and this was G-AEMW, a Cirrus-powered model. Resident at Elstree for some while it met its end at an airstrip at Clothall Common, Baldock, Hertfordhsire, on December 29th 1963 when it stalled on approach and ended up inverted.

American aircraft began to appear on the British register as early as 1936 but they were both expensive and costly to service. Richard Fairey of Fairey Aviation owned a Stinson Reliant SR-8B, G-AFMC registered in November that year but had the misfortune to crash it in September of 1939. G-AEOR was a replacement and it was used as a company communications machine during the early part of the war. However, by December of 1942 it became impossible to keep airworthy because of the non-availability of spares, so was scrapped at Ringway. Brian Allen Aviation Ltd had been the importer and in all five were brought into the country, the final three being impressed. The on-going spares problem affected all and they did not fly after the war. The curious starboard wing tip shape is because the aileron is fully up.

Pictured on February 1st 1946 at Gosselies in Belgium, Ernest O Tips flies his pre-war single-seat Tipsy S.1, OO-TIP. Here in Britain we were familiar with the two-seat S.2 with its curious slightly staggered side-by-side seats which saved several inches in overall fuselage width. Sadly, the S.1 did not fly again in post-war Britain. Survivors in the storehouse at the Slough factory of Tipsy, safely stored for five and more years, were now unceremoniously turned out and burned in an act of vandalism encouraged by the official policy of 'insufficient paperwork to reinstate any pre-war Permit to Fly status'.

Who remembers Harmondsworth? Perhaps better recalled as the Great West Aerodrome, it is today's London Heathrow Airport. Back in 1937, though, it was Fairey Aviation's new test aerodrome where, on May 14th, the Belgian-built Tipsy B would be demonstrated. The following month, Tipsy Aircraft Company Ltd would be formed by distributors Brian Allen, George Birkett, Leslie Irwin, Gilbert Miller and Major J E D Shaw. With a capital of £20,000 the new firm took over the former premises of Broughton-Blayney Aircraft Co at Hanworth and prepared to put the all-wood two-seater into production. The business of Ernest Oscar Tips ((1893-1948) was actually Avions Fairey, the Belgian subsidiary of Richard Fairey's Hayes company. By agreement, Tipsy was a closely-connected but separate business. Soon a larger factory was set up in Slough and production got going. The Tipsy B.2 with its Mikron engine was an immediate success but war intervened and work ceased. Happily a number of aircraft survived the war years and some incredibly still fly today. G-AFJT pictured here was built in 1938 and in 1950 romped into first place at that year's Grosvenor Challenge Cup race staged at Wolverhampton Aerodrome, the old Halfpenny Green. On August 23rd 1950, G-AFJT was sold to Finland where it became OH-SVA. Major John Edward Durrant Shaw (1894-1955) was an early owner of this particular Tipsy. It was he who would go on to finance Slingsby Sailplanes in the post-war years.

The Tipsy Trainer was built under licence at Slough in 1939, and G-AFWT, pictured here, got its C of A on August 5th that year – four weeks before all private flying was banned for the duration. It was restored to West London Aero Services Ltd at White Waltham in 1951 and later served with Old Warden's Home Counties Flying Group. Powered by a 62 hp Walter Mikron four-cylinder in-line engine, the two-seat all-wood aircraft only weighed 1,073 lb all-up and had a comfortable cruising speed of 100 mph. *Picture by M G Sweet.*

An aeroplane with an unwarranted miserable history was Ernest Oscar Tips' delightful single-seat Tipsy S. Designed and built at Gosselies in Belgium, Tipsy Aircraft was the sister company of Fairey Aviation and opened a British branch at Slough just before the war. Here it began building the two-seat Tipsy Trainer, a number of which came onto the market and survived the war to fly again. When 1946 came, the former Tipsy company decided that it was no longer viable to have a UK arm and so all its stock of existing airframes including some complete and almost complete airframes, were turfed out and burned. This vandalism was quite unjustified, but one has to remember that in 1946 it was an uphill task to try to fly an aircraft for which the right paperwork had been lost or did not exist. Here is a rare picture of G-AESU, one of those single-seat monoplanes. The legend on the nose reads 'Wards of Wallasey / Demonstrating the Tipsy'. Eric Darwent Ward of Wallasey, Cheshire, took delivery of the aeroplane from the Fairey Aviation Co. Ltd at Harmondsworth, on April 28th 1937. Tipsy, G-AESU, had been built earlier in the year by Aero Engines Ltd. at Kingswood, Bristol, Gloucestershire, and was fitted with a Douglas Sprite II 24 hp making it the first Tipsy to be fitted with a dual ignition. Ward would keep the Tipsy at Hooton Park Aerodrome, but it was a short-lived relationship for it was destroyed in a confrontation with trees on take-off at Walsall just six days later. Pilot Ward was unhurt and, on May 19th 1937, he took delivery of Tispy S.2 G-AEXK as a replacement. Ward must have lost his love of the brand very quickly for this aircraft was scrapped at Hooton that August. In the background of this snapshot stands the Gipsy I-powered DH.60G, G-ABJJ. This fared better: it went to Canada as CF-AAA and is now back flying in British skies.

One of the more interesting survivors of the war was the antiquated-looking wire-braced Aeronca 100. Unsuitable for impressment, this had been squirreled away out of harm's way and of the ones built at Peterborough pre-war – and a few that had been imported – most of the 20 or so that existed came out of hiding. The tale of the manufacturers, The Aeronautical Corporation of Great Britain Ltd based at the Walton Works, Sages Lane, Peterborough, is related in the book *British Light Aeroplanes… 1920-1940.* Suffice to say that it makes sad reading. Founded on April 15th 1936 and in voluntary liquidation on November 5th 1937, the Aeronca business was bedizened by poor and unpopular management, confrontational shareholders and financial deceit. Its innocent partners were engine-makers J A Prestwick (which laid down 120 engines – far short of a break-even number) and Arthur Alexander Dashwood Lang's Lang Propellers Ltd, both of which were lucky to survive the financial collapse of the parent company. The sales arm was Aircraft Exchange & Mart at Hanworth. Building this American design in Britain was an attempt to avoid the huge 30% sales tax on imported aircraft. By the time the original C.3 had been re-engineered to British standards and materials, the sale price was to be £395, but actual sales fell dramatically short of the firm's wild estimate of 200 per year. After the Northamptonshire firm had failed, the Hanworth distributors advertised aircraft at £245 and then, in May 1939, £145. They still didn't sell. G-AESP was the second of 19 British-built Aeronca 100 two-seaters. It was owned after the war by Arthur Robert 'Tiny' Pilgrim at Elstree but broken for spares in 1959. Other examples still fly today.

The Moss family was one of the more unusual among the pre-war aircraft manufacturers. The five Moss brothers were all avid flyers. Three held commissions in the Reserve of Air Force Officers and two held commercial pilot's licences. All were licensed flying instructors. The family business was H A Moss & Company, varnish manufacturers of Chorley, Lancashire. The brothers decided to design and build their own aircraft and on January 1st 1936, they registered a new company – Moss Brothers Aircraft Ltd. Their first project was a tandem two-seat low-winged sporting monoplane powered by a 95 hp Pobjoy Niagara. Of all-wood construction, the MA.1 Mosscraft had a closed cockpit, but in 1938 was revised with the unusual cockpit access system seen here whereby the complete fuselage top area together with windscreen, could be hinged to the starboard side to give full-width access. Pictured at Heston pre-war parked close to the fuel-pump bund. Note the extended mass-balance weight above the aileron. Stored between 1939 and 1945, it was quickly returned to the air and with the rear cockpit faired over it flew in the 1949 and 1950 King's Cup Races, William H Moss being the pilot. He was the pilot at Wolverhampton (Pendeford) Airport on June 17th 1950, and was killed during the race that day when the MA.1 crashed at the Newport, Shropshire turn.

Moss Brothers produced two delightful low-wing monoplanes – the Moss MA.1 and MA.2. For the historian, descriptions such as open cockpit and cabin are confused when talking about these machines, for they each appeared in differing guises. The MA.2 G-AFMS was first shown the May 1939 as an open tandem two-seater but in 1940 was converted into a cabin aircraft. The MA.1 G-AEST, on the other hand, was built as a cabin monoplane before being converted to an open two-seater with hinged cockpit coaming. It was then converted to an open cockpit two-seater and, later, with the rear cockpit faired over, as a single-seater. Here it is in its cabin days. The aircraft was lost in a crash at Newport Shropshire, during the 1950 King's Cup Race.

Designed and built at Heston before the war, the Heston Phoenix was an early attempt to produce an executive aircraft. The 200 hp Gipsy VI-powered all-wood high-wing had a lot going for it, not the least of which was a retractable undercarriage. At that time, folding wheels were both a rarity and a number-one selling-point. Six were built, including one for the Australian racing pilot, C J Jimmy Melrose. After the war, during which two had been impressed, only G-AESV remained and was sold at the great aircraft disposals auction held at Kemble in 1946. It was subsequently bought by Arthur Robert 'Tiny' Pilgrim who kept it at Elstree and, later, Bembridge. In April 1952, Pilgrim was flying the aircraft across the French Alps in poor visibility when he crashed into a peak. Although the machine was only slightly damaged it was impossible to salvage. Another pre-war type went extinct.

Designed in Czechoslovakia by Jaroslav Šlechta for the Czech National Flying Club Competition, first flown in September 1934 and then demonstrated at the 1934 Paris Salon, the Praga E.114 Air Baby was later manufactured under licence in Britain by F Hills & Son in Manchester. Known here as the Hillson Praga, it was a shoulder-wing all-wood sports aircraft which sat two side-by-side in a rather basic cabin which also formed the leading edge of the one-piece cantilever wing. Originally powered by a two-cylinder engine copied from the American Aeronca E.113C, later models had a four-cylinder flat four, still maintaining many of the features of the original twin including the exposed front of the crankcase which aided oil-cooling, and a Y-shaped exhaust pipe. The Praga B engines manufactured in Britain by Jowett Cars Ltd could not be certified for full C of A. At least five were replaced by the lower-powered and heavier 37 hp Aeronca JAP J-99 flat twin. It was a Praga that won the Manx Air Derby, flying three circuits of the Isle of Man on June 1st 1936, at 89.5 mph. In 1946 it was found that there were several Pragas still around and airworthy having been decided unsuitable for wartime impressment. These flew the peacetime skies, the last being this one, G-AEUT, first registered in January 1938 and surviving until being destroyed in a take-off mishap at Sinalunga, Siena, Italy, on June 19th 1957, when, following a forced landing, it struck trees.

The Percival Mew Gull G-AEXF was a popular racer after the war but the poor visibility from the cockpit resulted in a number of crashes on landing. Each time rebuilt, at one stage it appeared with a huge bulbous canopy. Here it is in happier days, but less its tight-fitting wheel spats that were originally so tight fitting that the aircraft could not be pushed backwards: the rubber air seals between spat and tyre became trapped in the tiny space available to them and had to be trimmed back.

In its post-war hey-days, the Mew Gull was a hark-back to the excitement of pre-war racing and long distance flight. A look in the cockpit made it hard to visualise that this machine had been used on Alex Henshaw's amazing out-and-home Cape record, the more so since the cockpit was so extremely small and cramped, not to mention the fact that the view forwards was virtually nothing. The author managed to sit inside this aircraft but could not stretch his legs. What it must have been like for a really long-distance flight can only be imagined.

The Percival Mew Gull was an incredibly sleek racer but, like so many of its breed, cockpit visibility, especially on the ground, was extremely poor. Originally ZS-AHM, G-AEXF had been raced extensively and, in post-war years, crashed rather more times than most. After one of its rebuilds, it emerged with this ugly raised cockpit which, while improving the view from the pilot's seat, did nothing for the overall top speed. Fortunately it was later restored to its sleek original lines.

This Dart Kitten G-AEXT belonged to W G 'Bill' Harrison who owned a garage on the A.40 just south of High Wycombe. He kept this machine at Booker. Inside his garage, on top of an inside office, was a complete set of parts for a second Kitten which somebody had acquired from Dart Aircraft in 1939 and hidden away 'for the duration'. These were later retrieved and, in 1952, appeared as a brand new Kitten, G-AMJP. G-AEXT had several nasty crashes throughout its post-war life but each time has been repaired and returned to the skies. One of these rebuilds took place in Evelyn Drive, Hatch End where the author kept Luton Minors and Aeroncas.

An advanced design for the 1930s was that of the Airspeed AS.6 Envoy of which at least one, G-AEXX – an Envoy Mk.III –survived to fly in post-war skies. Originally in the King's Flight in 1937, this richly-painted aircraft flew for the Royal Household in the red and blue livery of the Guards before assuming the marks L7270 in 1939. It was made airworthy again at Hanworth in 1946 and restored to George Farquharson who kept it for a year before selling it to Sweden as SE-ASN.

At one time it was 'politically correct' to describe a task as 'so simple even a woman can do it'. Those sentiments have never really been true as many examples (of which Amy Johnson is just one) have proved. But when de Havilland Aircraft at Hatfield wanted to show how simple it was to fold the wings of their new DH.94 Moth Minor prototype E.8 in 1937, this is the path they took. Expensive at £575 ex-works, a useful number or Moth Minors survived the war to form a useful private owner and club type. There were two forms – open cockpit and cabin variants.

A hark-back to 1941 as a DH.84 Moth Minor Coupé in wartime civilian markings. Very few of the cabin-top Moth Minors were made and this one, first flown two months before the outbreak of war, flew all through the conflict as a communications machine. Restored in 1946 it is still flying today. Note the red white and blue bands under the fuselage registration and the fin flash.

Luton Minor G-AFIR at Luton Airport standing next to Vivian Bellamy's beautiful DH.86 Express four-engined biplane in the summer of 1958. This is the Luton Minor which succeeded in breaking the Ministry of Aviation's policy of not even contemplating issuing a Permit to Fly to an aircraft that was registered pre-war, now completely rebuilt and with a new engine. As for the big biplane, it was written off at Madrid Airport less than a month after this picture was taken. A heavy landing cracked the rear spar and it was considered uneconomic to bring it home for repair. And so the last airworthy '86 went the way of all flesh.

One survivor of the war years was the Taylor-Watkinson Ding-Bat designed and built at Teddington, Middlesex, in 1938 by Eric T Watkinson and Cyril W Taylor. A low-wing monoplane powered by a 30 hp Carden-Ford engine, this single-seat ultra-light was inspired by the contemporary Chilton Monoplane and was more or less the same size. However, although the two men got Ranald Porteous, test pilot of the Chilton, to make the first flight at Heston in June 1938, it was soon obvious that it was no match for the Hungerford original. Lack of streamlining and the choice of a constant-chord wing all contributed to give the Ding-Bat a disappointing performance. Stored during the war it was donated to the Experimental Group of the ULAA at Elstree where it underwent a long-term rebuild. With a length of 16 feet and a span of 28 feet, the wing area was 125 sq.ft. Eventually it flew again in 1959 but a crash in 1975 set it back on another long-term rebuild.

In 1947, the Experimental Group of the Ultra Light Aicraft Association at Elstree was given this unique Taylor-Watkinson Ding-Bat, G-AFJA. It was a very long time being restored to flying condition but did indeed grace the peaceful skies that closed the 20th century. Carden-Ford-powered, it retained its original pre-war colour scheme – light blue and white.

The Ding-Bat was finally restored to flying condition in 1959 and is seen here at a Popular Flying Association Rally. While the limited power of the very heavy Carden-Ford engine managed to give a diminutive Chilton Monoplane a good performance and turn of speed, the high-drag Ding-Bat struggled with the engine. The designers were practical men who just failed to appreciate that the secret of success with 30 dubious horsepower lay in detail and refinement – and a good wing shape.

The Ding-Bat was first registered in August of 1938. After the war it ended up at Elstree with the Experimental Group of the Ultra Light Aircraft Association. The author spent many hours on this simple little aircraft renewing plywood repeatedly broken by people (so-called 'spotters') stepping on the wing to look inside the cockpit. But we never completed it and it was taken to Redhill where it languished for yet more years. Ultimately it was restored to flying condition. These pictures, taken at a PFA Rally, show how different it was to the infinitely better contemporary – the Chilton DW.1. The wide-track undercarriage made it tricky to handle on rough grass, even with a tailskid.

The prototype Chilton DW.1, G-AESZ first flew in 1937 and was an eager returner to peacetime skies. It underwent a sympathetic rebuild to ensure that it will fly for a while yet. All-red fuselage and high-gloss silver wings, the Chiltons were all meticulously manufactured and the wing trailing edges were so finely shaped that it was said that one might shave with them. This was an exaggeration, but the message was clear. Here is a recent picture of the aircraft on the lawn at Chilton, Hungerford, where it was originally built. An amusing incident occurred in 1948 involving this machine. Ranold Porteous, the famed Auster test pilot who in pre-war days had made the very first Chilton flight, bought DW.1A G-AFGH but soon afterwards sold it to the owner of Denham Aerodrome, Dr John Miles Bickerton. Entered for the 1949 King's Cup Race, there was consternation when Bickerton seriously damaged his G-AFGH in a forced landing at South Chalfont on July 3rd. G-AESZ was at that time dismantled for overhaul and Denham Aero Club engineer Vickie Nightscale had the notion of quickly assembling G-AFGH's wings to G-AESF's fuselage so it could take part in the race. The race took part in time for Sqdn Ldr H R Bilborough to fly it in the Grosvenor Cup Race. He only managed 13th at 95.5 mph – but the aircraft gave observers some fun with its identity. Naturally, all was subsequently returned to normal and the Chiltons fly as intended today.

The Chilton DW.1A G-AFSV was a popular star at many post-war air shows and, as testimony to something about keeping a good aeroplane down, it is still flying today. Here it is pictured flying near Booker in 1969. The name on the side reads 'Barbara Ann III', a title that inspires a host of questions in the minds of the curious!

The single-seat Chilton DW.1 was designed by two former de Havilland Technical School students, the Hon Andrew William Henry Dalrymple (1914-46), and Alexander Reginald Ward (1915-87). Both were also Old Etonians. Constructed in outbuildings at Chilton Lodge, Hungerford, the prototype, G-AESZ, first flew in 1937 in the hands of Ranald Logan Porteous (1916-98) and was powered by a Carden-Ford 32hp engine. Priced at £315 ex-works, four were built before the war and all survived with several replicas being made in recent years. Here is a fine picture of the first machine parked on the lawn outside the family home, Chilton Lodge which was designed by Sir William Pilkington and built between 1798 and 1801 to replace an earlier structure. The spacious gardens of this jewel of a house were laid out by the great Humphrey Repton. It was after a Christmas Day party at this family seat in 1946 that the Hon Dalrymple lost his life when he went flying from the lawn in a captured German Fiesler Storch aircraft. It turned out to have been sabotaged before capture and aileron failure finally put paid to the post-war hopes of Chilton Aircraft Ltd. The picture was taken on August 13th 1999.

Five Chiltons were projected – G-AESZ (prototype), G-AFGH, G-AFGI, G-AFSV and G-AFSW. The first four were completed but the outbreak of war put the brakes on the last-mentioned aircraft after the airframe was three-quarters complete. The other four models – three DW.1 models and G-AFSV classified a DW.1A, were completed and flew. They were fast and manoeuvrable. None ever experienced a serious accident although G-AFGI suffered some damage shortly before one of the King's Cup Races as a result of which, and as recounted earlier, it flew with the wings of G-AFGH – confusing a wagonload of spotters. The unfinished G-AFSW donated its components over the years to keep the rest of the fleet flying. The one shown here was first registered on October 20th 1938, and has been a regular at air shows throughout the post-war era.

Geoffrey N Wikner was the brother-in-law of Edgar Percival of Percival Aircraft. Both were Australian-born. He came to England in May 1934, with the notion of building aircraft to his own design. He teamed up with two other men, V Foster and J F Lusty and formed Foster Wikner Aircraft Ltd with a factory in the corner of Lusty's furniture factory in Bromley-by-Bow. Originally, Wikner wanted to fit a Ford car engine to his aircraft. The prototype aircraft did indeed fly with this somewhat heavy motor, but the authorities would not approve it for a saleable aircraft so forcing his hand to use Blackburn Cirrus and de Havilland engines. The company's Wicko monoplane emerged just before the outbreak of war. Only G-AFJB survived the bad years and, happily, is still flying. Here it is pictured at Popham in 2012.

One of the regular participants in post-war air displays was Hawker Tomtit G-AFTA which, during the war years, was test pilot Alex Henshaw's personal mount based at the Castle Bromwich Aeroplane Factory where many Spitfires were produced. Also flown by Neville Duke, this one was also fitted with a Spitfire front screen. With its 155 hp Armstrong Siddeley Mongoose radial engine, this dark blue and white two-seater was also one of Hawker's first all-metal biplanes. Although still fabric-covered it marked a great leap in both faith and development for the Kingston-on-Thames factory. After a few changes of ownership, Hawker Aircraft bought the aircraft in July 1950 and restored it to pristine condition and based it at Dunsfold. Later repainted in its one-time original RAF colours as K1786, it now resides with the Shuttleworth Trust at Old Warden.

The day of the Elstree Air Rally – September 5th 1948 – and Robert H Parker arrives at the aerodrome towing his dismantled Heath Parasol, G-AFZE, behind his car all the way from his South London home. That afternoon was spent erecting the machine before the admiring and inquisitive eyes of the spectators. *Picture by courtesy of John Berkeley.*

Bob Parker ultimately sold G-AFZE to Frank G Lowe who took it to Croydon and fitted it with a 32 hp Bristol Cherub III flat twin which was more than double the power output of the original Blackburne Tomtit V-twin of just 670cc originally installed. The silver and red Parasol crashed at Luton on May 1st 1966 and was being rebuilt by Kenneth Cortaine Desmond St Cyrien who had hoped to fly again in 1978. Left derelict for a number of years after the owner's death, it is currently once more under restoration. In its original form it is pictured here at Elstree back in 1948.

Bob Parker began building his Heath Parasol in 1936 and had it registered before the war. On its post-war completion he had been assured he would get a Permit to Fly because he had not altered anything since his pre-war specification. On September 11th, it was ready for first trials at Elstree with test pilot Colin H Debenham in the cockpit. It wouldn't get airborne. Then followed trials with a succession of different propellers to try to gain that 'sweet-spot' combination of engine revs and thrust. More trials on November 6th elicited the same result. On November 20th, however, the aircraft managed to fly several yards at several inches altitude. More propeller experiments coincided with a period of heavy rain and thick fog that lasted until Christmas. Not until the morning of January 9th 1949 could trials resume. A flight at several feet extending the full length of the runway was now made and, after lunch, Debenham attempted a circuit – and succeeded. It was a between-the-trees type of flight but it was flight and Parker was jubilant. That evening the popular radio comic Tommy Handley, who had made us laugh all through the war, died aged just 55. Parker and Debenham then arranged a press conference for January 16th when everybody turned up to film events. One of the images taken was this one. Somebody forgot to remind Parker of the safety rule about never moving an aircraft unless the prop is horizontal… That was the year Neville Duke won the Kemsley Air Trophy in Comper Swift G-ABUS on August 1st.

The original Blackburne Tomtit engine had been designed for the Lympne Light Aeroplane trials by Burney and Blackburne Limited at Bookham, Surrey. With a capacity of 670cc, this V-twin former motorcycle engine was rated at about 20 hp. It was patently obvious that G-AFZE was underpowered with the Tomtit engine so a Bristol Cherub which turned out between 32 and 34 hp was fitted and this made all the difference. Here is the aircraft being run up with its new power unit. Now that flight was possible with some ease, it highlighted the problem regarding the small tail. Under ideal conditions it was big enough but the margin for error was too small. The author was asked to do something about it…

This picture was taken after the tail had been enlarged to cure a tendency to wander due to insufficient control. With its new and larger tail having an increased fin and rudder area, the rudder with an aerodynamic balance, plus a larger tailplane and elevators, it now flew somewhat better. Here it is pictured at Finningley. The new tail was just right. The Parasol enjoyed occasional flying and was based at Luton Aerodrome in the 1960s. On April 1st 1966, it crashed into a perimeter fence and was badly damaged. It is currently being restored.

A second Heath Parasol, G-AJCK, was built at Christchurch by the South Hants Ultra Light Aeroplane Club in 1948. This was initially fitted with a 30 hp ABC Scorpion but was later re-engined with 40 hp Aeronca JAP flat twin. Owned by Roger A Mann, it first flew in 1949 but crashed sometime in 1953.

Heath Parasol G-AJCK was fitted with a 30 hp ABC Scorpion. The Authorisation to Fly was granted on January 15th 1949 and first flight attempts were undertaken by the Airspeed test pilot, George Errington. It was subsequently sold to the Airways Aero Association at Hurn where it was fitted with the J.99 JAP flat twin as seen here in the picture taken at White Waltham on May 14th 1950. This aircraft flew successfully until 1953 when it was written off in an accident.

Errol Spencer Shapley of Torquay, Devon, designed a successful open-cockpit single-seater of unusual gull-wing design in the late 1930s and then went on to create a Pobjoy-powered cabin two-seater from this prototype. G-AFRP had flown in 1939. Stored throughout the war, now was the time to bring it to fruition and ultimate production. The Kittiwake II was a tubby aircraft – some said it was like a flying barrel – but it had excellent handling qualities including a 90-yard take-off and a rate of climb of 920 ft/min. Fully aerobatic and with a good turn of speed, Kittiwake II was a thoroughly promising design. In May 1946, Shapley was ready to embark on air tests to qualify for a Certificate of Airworthiness prior to production. An 'approved' test pilot was involved. All went swimmingly well until, on May 10th, tests involving maximum aft C of G were being made. Unfortunately the pilot forgot to ascertain that the rear fuel tank was empty: it was not. This meant the C of G was much further aft than intended. At a height of 18,000 feet the aircraft was undergoing stall tests when it developed an inverted flat spin. This could very easily be corrected, especially with so much height to play with. Instead the pilot chose to bail out. G-AFRP was destroyed in the subsequent crash and, Shapley was so disillusioned that he gave up the project and flying, emigrated and became a farmer.

As we have just seen, some aeroplanes, intended as post-war revivalists, failed. This was the fate of the C W Cygnet, an all-metal cabin two-seater. Designed in 1936 by Carl R Chronander and James I Waddington who traded as C W Aircraft, this was, for its time, a quite advanced aircraft. They advertised it for sale at £1,200 but its designers had insufficient funds to develop it to production so the business was bought out by General Aircraft Ltd, the Monospar builders at Hanworth. Great plans were made for mass-production and when the war broke out, General Aircraft continued promoting the Cygnet well into 1940 before it became apparent to all that the war had a while to run. Meanwhile ten aircraft were made, the prototype tailwheel aircraft with single fin and rudder changed to the Mark 2 version with a tricycle undercarriage and twin tail. Seven aircraft appeared on the British civil register, the other three being unfinished. No attempt was made to restart production after the war was over. However, six had survived to fly again including this one, G-AGAX, which finally crashed near Barnsley, Yorkshire, on April 4th 1955. While the Cygnet was nice to fly, lack of any cabin insulation meant that it suffered from extreme cockpit noise. In-flight conversation with your passenger was thus a no-no.

The Austrian-built Hirtenberg HS.9 was a parasol monoplane powered by a 120 hp de Havilland Gipsy I engine. The product of the Hirtenberger Patronen Zündhutchen Metallwarenfabriek AG, this seems to have been the sole example built. Thought to have been made as a demonstrator, it was first registered OE-DJH and taken to Germany where it was re-registered D-EDJH. In July 1939 it flew to England but there was some confusion over its paperwork and it was 'detained'. Meanwhile it was re-registered G-AGAK but, with the outbreak of war less than six weeks away, the aircraft 'disappeared' into storage. A J Jackson says that this was at Filton but one cannot be sure. What is certain is that in the summer of 1946 it arrived at Gatwick by road and was overhauled for J H Davis – the man originally involved in its importation pre-war. Later its owner was Jack Cosmelli and it was a familiar sight at Elstree. Despite its cumbersome appearance, it was a delight to fly and featured full-span ailerons. One day, while en route to Bembridge the aircraft encountered poor visibility or what was known locally as 'an Arundel fog'. Jack was earnestly looking out for the ground on the left-hand side of the aircraft when the right-hand side flew into Butser Hill, Petersfield. Jack survived the impact but the venerable Hirtenberg did not.

The Benes Mraz BE.161 Bibi, G-AGSR, was built at Chocen, Czechoslavakia, in 1937. Serial Numbered 2 and first registered OK-BET, it was an all-wood two-seater designed by Pavel Benes and Jaroslav Mraz. While resembling a Percival Vega Gull, it was a good bit smaller and its power unit was the diminutive and lightweight 62 hp Walter Mikron inline four-cylinder engine. Flown to Croydon in 1938 under obscure circumstances (it was supposed to have been 'imported' but it was more likely to have been associated with the escape of a young Jewish pilot and his wife), it was stored during the war, taking its British registration and C of A on July 30th 1945. It was finished in cream yellow with a crimson cheat line and black registration. Acquired by veteran private pilot H Clive-Smith (who had owned Avro Avian G-ABPU in 1931) it was hangared with the Experimental Group of the Ultra Light Aircraft Association at Elstree where members worked steadily to restore the aircraft after its years in storage. Finally it was sold to N C Chorlton in May 1950 who based it at White Waltham. Following overhaul for C of A renewal, it went for air-test on October 25th 1951. During servicing, the aileron cables were inadvertently crossed. The pilot was killed and a fine and rare aircraft which was a true delight to fly was no more.

The Portsmouth Aerocar G-AGTG, first flown on June 18th 1947, was a classic example of a wasted opportunity. Britain desperately needed capital from sales of exported goods and the Aerocar was a first-rate candidate for overseas sales not to mention having a healthy order-book of home sales. The problem was finance to fund manufacturing and Portsmouth Aviation, just surviving after the years of the war, needed money to develop. Nothing was forthcoming and the government of the time would not help. Projected manufacturing tie-ups with other aircraft-makers, predominantly Auster and Miles, were not forthcoming so the Aerocar with its two 155 hp Blackburn Cirrus Major III engines was allowed to fade. A first-rate aeroplane that had everything going for it, not the least of which was a bunch of orders that many makers would give their eye teeth for, was allowed to disappear. In 1950 the scrap-men cut up an aircraft that was fully tested and universally lauded. It would not be the first time such stupidity would rob us of a fine aeroplane. The design was technically very advanced for its time.

G-AGOH was a historic Auster. Confusingly, the prototype Autocrat had been built out of surplus parts which included an old Auster 5 fuselage with a new engine – the 100 hp Blackburn Cirrus Minor 2. First flown on October 8th 1945, this hybrid put in half a century of service before its days were up. Last flown in the mid 1990s, it is today in Newark Air Museum.

An Autocrat by any other name, the extended cabin windows of the '5' brand this as a rather non-standard prototype. Still flying until 1997, it is now a museum exhibit having given more than half a century of yeoman service. Stemming from the Army Auster of wartime production, the Taylorcraft design team was not alone in seeing a potential for its two-seater in the latter stages of the Second World War. The consequence was that plans were made for a lower-powered version of the military Auster 5. The engine would be the 100 hp Blackburn Cirrus Minor 2 and so, in April of 1945, the first civil aircraft to emerge from the Leicester factory of Taylorcraft was the Auster J-1 Autocrat.

The prototype Auster Autocrat G-AGOH was built from the crashed remains of the prototype Taylorcraft Plus D first built in 1939 and registered then as G-AFWN. The remains were taken out of storage and rebuilt with the 'new' fuselage of an Auster 5 to create the three-seat J-1. The Rearsby product would be more expensive than government-surplus aircraft such as Tiger Moths which, assuming the average cost of purchase plus civil registration bringing it to Certificate of Airworthiness standard was only between £400 and £500. The Autocrat cost £1,200, a price which would rise to almost £1,500. Nevertheless, it had its followers and gradually the flying clubs and private owners saw the benefits of a new cabin aircraft over a reconditioned open cockpit.

Elstree Flying Club began in the immediate post-war years as the United Services Aero Club, part of London Aero & Motor Services, the holding company which operated Elstree Aerodrome. Until 1939 the field was known as Aldenham Airport. The club started out with Austers and here, outside the big hangar which during the war housed military aircraft that were being serviced and repaired, stand the first of the club's machines – G-AGVT, G-AGXT and G-AGXJ, all painted in the club's orange and black livery.

The National Air Races staged at Elmdon in 1949 provided spectacle and excitement for both participants and spectators. Here a Miles Gemini, G-AKGE, entered by the Goodyear Tyre & Rubber Company, flies flat out across the Birmingham airfield.

The thrills of air-racing entertained many, especially at those events that involved coastal flying when sun-bathing, sand-castles and a bit of air entertainment were the fodder of the post-war holidaymakers. Here Miles Gemini 1A G-AKKG chases Miles M.38 Messenger painted up to resemble RG333, the second of two prototypes which Miles Aircraft built as an unauthorised private venture during the war, getting a sound reprimand from the Ministry of Aircraft Production for their labours – and then a good solid order for military use! In fact, the original RG333 belonged to the 2nd TAF Communications Squadron, RAF, and was written off in a landing accident at Oldenberg in Lower Saxony on August 22nd 1945. The imposter, seen here, is actually G-AIEK flying in unauthorised colours.

A little too close for comfort in the days before 'health and safety' tended to sterilise air-displays and move racing lines into the region of spectator binoculars! A Miles Messenger races flat out very close to the public enclosure line, left, as the Arrow Active, G-ABVE, catches up at a slightly greater height. A scene from a post-war air-race.

April 1953 was not a happy one in terms of private flying. Tom Hayhow disappeared on April 10th and his remains and those of his aircraft would not be found until May 25th. But there was another loss that month. Miles Messenger G-AKBL had first been registered on August 20th 1947 and served three years with Smithfield Refrigerator Co Ltd at Elstree as their company runabout until March 1950 when it was sold to Ireland as EI-AFH. Comprehensively restored at Elstree in February 1953, it was owned by the notable private and racing pilot, 35-year-old Australian-born Rodney Richard Matthews-Naper at County Meath. A farmer by profession and owner of an estate at Loughcrew, Oldcastle, he was a great sportsman who took part in many races. On September 28th 1952, he had organised a rally at Dunmore East, County Waterford, which was widely attended by pilots from north and south of the border. At 6.40 pm on April 1st 1953, he took off from Northolt to fly to Dublin. On board with him was Walter Bradley. Apart from R/T contact with Dublin at 9.50 pm, nothing further was ever heard from him. A widespread and prolonged search failed to find any trace. He had used his Messenger widely for business and pleasure and at the time of his disappearance was planning to fly it to Australia.

Bedsides the great numbers of Tiger Moths and Magisters available as government surplus was a number of Percival Proctors. These were, at the time, considered big for the private owner and, with their Gipsy Queen engines, very thirsty, meaning expensive to run. True, they were powerful but they were also fast and fairly comfortable so if you had the money you flew one. They also made useful company aircraft and this one, G-AGTC a Proctor V, was used by Hunting Aircraft Ltd. This aircraft lasted a useful 24 years until May 2nd 1969, when a forced landing on the beach near Malaga Airport proved its undoing.

The story of the Sponson Tribian is a long and involved one related in detail in the author's book *British Private Aircraft 1946-70 – An A To Z of Club & Private Aircraft*. Suffice to say here that the Redhill Aerodrome-based Tiltman Langley Laboratories and Sponson Developments Ltd had great hopes for this unusual twin-engined amphibian. Sales director of Sponson was The Hon Simon George Warrender (1922-2011). He bought a Percival Proctor G-AGSW and set off for Australia on May 17th 1951 ostensibly to undertake a sales tour for the Tribian with a secondary brief from Percival Aircraft Ltd at Luton to sell Proctors. He took 34 days to get to Melbourne where he sold the aircraft, pictured here before the flight, which became VH-ADP on July 17th 1951. Warrender had a girlfriend in Australia and soon he was married into the influential Myer family. The role of down-under socialites subsumed the newly-weds and, apart from much later assisting Freddie Laker in trying to fly his airline there, his aviation days were over and the loser was the Tribian, never to see the light of day – apart from an abandoned Redhill wall-mounted mock-up, that is.

Developed directly from the single-engined Miles Messenger, the twin-engined Gemini used the same wing as the earlier model. It was the first light twin suitable for the private owner and sporting pilot. Interestingly, Miles sold 79 Messengers compared with 97 Geminis – a result which appeals to economists as well as numerologists! G-AKFY was registered on September 10th 1947. That December, it went to Switzerland as HB-EEF where it remained for two years. Restored to British ownership in March of 1949 it was finally scrapped at Biggin Hill in November 1963.

From the Envoy, the Airspeed company developed the Oxford which was used extensively during the war as a twin-engined trainer. In 1946, Airspeed at Portsmouth took more than 150 surplus Oxford airframes and converted them into light civil transports as the AS.65 Consul. Simple and easy to fly, they were a boon to the many small and often one-man transport companies that, fondly calling themselves 'airlines', operated in the late 1940s. One of these aircraft was converted into a private flying ambulance and this was G-AJWR. Virtually identical to standard models the only major alteration was a large stretcher door in the port side. This got its C of A in July 1947 but that October was sold to France as F-BEDP. Operated by Société Indochinoise de Transports Aériens, it was badly damaged by fire at Saigon's Tan Son Nhat International Airport on November 26th 1950, and subsequently scrapped. Saigon is today's Ho Chi Minh. Incidentally, while Airspeed was converting surplus Oxfords at one side of Portsmouth Airport, Hants & Sussex Aviation Ltd at the other side was breaking up redundant examples of the same aircraft.

Back in the days when Luton was merely a municipal aerodrome with Percival Aircraft's factory, it also featured an active flying club. Auster J-1 Autocrat G-AGXH was one of its aircraft seen here parked between the hangars. Later converted to J-1N standard, this aircraft was finally to be found derelict at Lympne in December 1971.

A scene from Denham Aerodrome on June 29th 1955, on the occasion of a BBC Television outside broadcast showing a line-up of resident and visiting aircraft. From the left is the tail and wing of Auster Autocrat G-AHSN followed by the distinctive rounded tail of Gloster Gladiator G-AMRK. Then there is Hawker Tomtit G-AFTA, Avro Club Cadet G-ACHP, Blackburn B.2 G-AEBJ, DH.60 Moth G-ABLV (visiting from Hatfield), and finally the Vintage Flying Club's Spartan Arrow G-ABWP. Denham Aerodrome, originally known as Hawksridge Aerodrome, was a First World War landing ground but really began in 1933 when John Myles Bickerton acquired it and operated his DH.60G Moth, G-ABAG, from its turf. The Moth still flies.

After the Tiger Moth biplane, the RAF's other wartime *ab initio* trainer aircraft was the Miles M.14 Hawk Trainer Mk.III, better known as the Magister. Here is pre-war G-AFBS which saw service as BB661 and was restored to fly again in post-war years. Mistakenly allocated a 'new' registration, G-AKKU, it was quickly corrected and 'FBS triumphed again. The spurious registration was re-allocated to a Handley Page Halifax, RT892. For some reason, this Mk.9 was not converted and the troublesome registration lapsed.

The Miles Hawk Trainer III was used extensively during the war as an RAF *ab initio* trainer and this one, originally T9896, was registered G-AKRV on January 24th 1948. Named *Judith Anne*, this, together with its sister aircraft G-AKRW, was modified with an enclosed coupé cabin-top. Entered for the 1950 King's Cup Race, this was one of ten similar machines that competed at Wolverhampton on that day. Piloted by Edward Day, it won at 138.5 mph. Later sold as VP-KNW to Tanganyika, the Hawk had the misfortune to crash on March 22nd 1956. Here it is pictured at Shoreham on September 16th 1950.

Developed out of the Hawk III, this variant was George Miles' attempt at designing a replacement. G-AHKY was a Miles M.6 Hawk devised in the hope to gain an order for a trainer for the RAF as a substitute for the familiar Magister. Slightly sleeker than the earlier Miles Hawk III and with a much larger fin and rudder, just two examples were built and flown in post-war years – this and G-AHOA. A nice aircraft to fly, it nevertheless did not impress the RAF who did not order it partly because it was offered too late in the war. It made a good post-war flyer, though.

Panshanger Aerodrome was one of the high-spots for flying up to the end of the 20th century. This enormous L-shaped grass airfield almost wholly surrounded by open countryside yet close to Welwyn Garden City, served as a base for Mosquito maintenance at one time and in the immediate post-war years was the home of the de Havilland School of Flying. This picture dates from July 17th 1952, and shows a line-up of Hatfield products. The London Aeroplane Club Tiger Moth nearest the camera is G-ALIX, commonly nicknamed 'Tiger Licks'. Next to it is G-AHUB, then the veteran DH.60G Moth G-EBLV, and a couple more Tigers. Hornet Moth G-AEET shows its wings, left. Panshanger was recently snapped up by developers who erected an estate of cheap-looking houses on this hallowed turf despite valid protests from a very active aviation sector.

What makes a DH.82 a DH.82a is largely down to these screwed-on flat-topped aluminium fairings called anti-spin strakes. Originally these became mandatory on RAF training models of the venerable Tiger Moth and their usefulness extended to the Miles Hawk Trainer or Magister as the RAF version was called.

The immediate post-war years saw a lot of rather risqué flying best described as 'letting one's hair down'. Here at Panshanger in the autumn of 1949 Tiger Moth G-AHXC puts in a rather steep turn low over J-1 Autocrat G-AIKD. The Tiger later crashed at Hatfield (June 28th 1952) and the Auster was sold to France on January 13th 1950, becoming F-BEXT. Bottom far right is the long hut which was to become the headquarters of E A Gilbert's North London Aero Club, premises shared with the Hertfordshire Police Flying Club.

Large numbers of DH.82a Tiger Moths were released as government surplus from the end of the war right up into the 1950s when the last of the RAFVR Tiger Squadrons was re-equipped. G-AHXB was one of these, having originally been T5978 and first registered on March 17th 1954. This was still the age when our fragile national economy was dependent on foreign earnings so it was all-too eagerly sold on to New Zealand where it became ZK-BFL.

More from that quiet field at Hillington, King's Lynn in Norfolk where Tiger Moth G-AMEY stands with some fine shaped oak trees. Originally DE578, this aircraft had an unusual life. Having been 'written off' in a crash at Little Snoring on May 16th 1968, it was rebuilt as a replica Rumpler for use in a film before finally going the way of all unwanted aircraft in 1969. *Picture by M G Sweet.*

The de Havilland Tiger Moth was certainly the mainstay of post-war revival private and club flying. It was dirt-cheap to buy – usually between £25 and £50 – and it offered a wide possibility of modification to improve or otherwise enhance its fundamental specification. These alterations included cabin-tops or coupé conversions (rather like the Canadian standard DH.82C) and, in the case of the Thruxton Jackaroo, fairly extensive changes to make it into a four-seater. But it was also eminently suited to other roles such as crop-spraying and aerobatics. In the latter category, it was Norman Jones of the Tiger Club at Croydon who saw how the basic Tiger could be changed ever so slightly to become a performance aerobatist. His first soirée into this category was with G-APDZ registered on July 7th 1957. Modified as a single-seater with an inverted fuel system for sustained upside-down flight, this was named *The Bishop*. To improve its rate of role the anti-spin strakes which had been added to the original DH.82 were removed. This Moth was a star-turn at air shows at the end of the fifties but it met an unfortunately fatal end at Little Snoring on May 12th 1960 while practising aerobatics.

The Easter Monday crowds at Sywell Aerodrome on March 30th 1970, were entertained by the antics of the 'flying cowboy', 38-year-old Leicester garage proprietor Malcolm Major as he sped across the airfield sitting on the lower wing root of a Tiger Moth flown at a height of 20 feet by Mike Parker. His object was discharging his Colt revolver at balloons attached to a trailer. Entertaining for the spectators but rather questionable as time would suggest.

Wing-walking began in America where barnstorming pilots devised all manner of daredevil acts to attract visitors and their dollars. Quite often wing-walking was just that – walking along the wings of a biplane in flight. Occasionally people fell off, but it added to the drama of the event. Of course, such dangerous behaviour was prohibited in conservative Britain until the Tiger Club thought of a way round it. The upshot was a braced tubular steel frame rigidly attached to the aircraft upper wing centre-section. This mounted a robust harness so that the person strapped into the frame could not fall out. 'Wing-walking' British style comprised strapping some poor individual into place on the top wing of a Tiger Moth – usually a young lady for best effect – and having her wave her arms about. This variant on the original is incredibly safe and only if the aircraft turned over on landing would our intrepid artiste be at risk. Since she stands above the area of the propeller slipstream, and since Tigers don't go very fast at the best of times, it's a bit like standing on the sea front in a strong wind. Spectacular? Sort of. Dangerous? You decide!

Following on the success of the Tiger Club's sporting Tiger Moth *The Bishop* came G-ANZZ, *The Archbishop*. Like its forerunner, it dispensed with the centre-section top-wing fuel tank in favour of a wholly-new inverted fuel system and flew without the anti-spin strakes on the aft fuselage.

Another Tiger Moth with an interesting history was the Tiger Club's G-AIVW. Flown by the RAF as T5370, it took its C of A in December 1946, won the 1958 King's Cup air race at Baginton, and later, after a heavy landing had damaged the undercarriage, it was converted to a seaplane with two large floats. Its first flight as a seaplane took place on July 20th 1963 and it was subsequently based at Lee-on-Solent. After some years of operation, it suffered a bad crash and was written off.

The Tiger Club's G-AIVW became a seaplane following an alleged landing accident 'which bent the undercarriage' and left wide-open an opportunity to make what was then Britain's only operational floatplane. Fitted with the Edo floats removed from a scrapped Aeronca Sedan, it was based initially at Gosport and later at Scotney Court, also known as Jury's Gap, a licensed water aerodrome on the border between Kent & Sussex and 1.5 miles SW of Lydd. Soon after conversion to a waterplane in July 1963, salt-water corrosion was found in the rear fuselage. It was replaced by that of G-ANLR which had crashed at Syderstone near Fakenham in Norfolk in April 1966. G-AIVW flew satisfactorily for a long while until, on August 27th 1982, it crashed into the sea off Silver Sands.

Elstree Flying Club's Auster J-1 Autocrat G-AHCL flies parallel to Elstree Aerodrome's sole runway. Visible in this picture, the aircraft's starboard wheel is just over the old blister hangar which was used by the Experimental Group of the Ultra Light Aircraft Association from 1947. The shed in the right foreground was ground engineer 'Tubby' Simpson's home and the path running out of shot to the right leads to the main hangar where once London Aero & Motor Services kept their Handley Page Halifax transport aircraft and Halton G-AHZM saw out its days after an undercarriage collapse in September 1946. The whole area from the blister hangar to the left subsequently became a reservoir and the boundary farm track, visible in the foreground, the fields and the hedges were obliterated. Auster G-AHCL later became an Alpha and, in June 1983, was re-registered G-OJVC.

Of the many variants of Auster which stemmed from the original J-1 Autocrat, the J-5Q Alpine G-APDB pictured here was created using a J-5F fuselage and tail assembly combined with the J-5B Autocar wings fitted with improved F-5F ailerons. Finally the whole thing was driven by a 130 hp de Havilland Gipsy Major I powerplant. The Auster company was certainly creative over its years and ringing the changes on parts and components produced a wide variety of different types which not always resulted in readily-identifiable variants. G-APCB was first registered on June 6th, 1957, the first owners being Jack Heywood Ltd. In this picture it is preparing to take off from a field at Hillington, seven miles north-east of King's Lynn in Norfolk in 1966. *Picture by M G Sweet.*

Back in September 1946, this Auster Autocrat was registered G-AIBP but in May of 1952 it was sold to Queensland, Australia, becoming VH-ASI. Thus painted, it embarked on a solo delivery flight for which the range was increased by the fitment of a standard long-range belly tank, seen fitted here, and an extra fuel tank in the cockpit modelled on the chemical tank used in the J-1U Workmaster. The aircraft was successfully delivered.

Auster J-1U Workmaster was specially devised as a single-seat crop-sprayer with large wheels, and a big chemical tank next to the pilot. The present author was consultant designer for Austers. G-APMH was the second to be built and is seen here fitted with four self-contained Micronair rotary atomisers and was operated by Crop Culture (Aerial) Ltd, associate company of the original Britten-Norman Ltd at Bembridge on the Isle of Wight. After a colourful career working in the French colonies, it was restored as a 'normal' aircraft in January 1965 and operated by the Cornish Gliding Club at Perranporth from May 1970. It was written off in a crash at Trevallas, Cornwall, on December 22nd that year.

As the 1940s advanced we became more accustomed to seeing strange foreign-built aircraft in our skies and one of these was a delightful four-seater built in Copenhagen by Skandinavisk Aero Industri AS and called the KZ-VII Laerke or Lark. Aircraft dealers R K Dundas imported two examples in 1947, G-AJHM, pictured here, and G-AJZV. The latter example did not have a long life: three months after taking up British citizenship it crashed four miles north-west of Manston in Kent on December 20th. The one seen here had been OY-AAN and was owned by G J Dawson until it went to Guernsey and then, in July of 1949, to France at F-BFXA. Here it is pictured in 1948 with the tail of Proctor V G-AHTM in the background.

Designed by Richard C Christoforides, the Chrislea Ace series of aircraft were unconventional in their cockpit layout having a wheel instead of a control column. This wheel could be moved up and down, and from side to side as well as being rotated. The main criticism was that there was no obvious 'dead centre' position, something you had to find out for yourself as the aircraft gathered speed on the ground. There was no rudder bar or pedals either. Initially the works were at Heston but when that airport closed down in 1947, production was shifted to Exeter Airport where the Chrislea CH.3 Series 2 Super Ace was built, the first example being this one, G-AKFD. This made its first flight in February 1948 with a Gipsy Major 10 engine. A demonstration tour of flying clubs finally convinced its makers that having nothing on the floor but a carpet was not intuitive to the majority of pilots. The designers bowed to the pressure – and this machine was retro-fitted with a rudder bar. You still had to cope with the wheel, though.

G-AKVF, serial number 114, was a Chrislea CH.3 Super Ace first registered in March 1948. The Ace is remembered for its unconventional control system which was a wheel on a shaft which itself moved up and down and sideways. The early examples did not have a rudder bar, all control operations being conducted with the wheel on its free moving shaft. As explained earlier, the problem was that there was no 'centre point' in the system so you were never quite sure how the controls were until you were moving fast enough to be able to move the wheel to correct unwanted deviation. An early change was to accept that many pilots found this too difficult – imprecise would be a better word – and so a rudder bar was added. However, the Ace's wheel remained and it became the Marmite feature. Some found it delightful and simple while others could not abide it.

After the Ace and the Super Ace on their three-wheeled landing gear, the more conventional Skyjeep appeared. First shown at the Royal Aeronautical Society garden party staged at White Waltham on May 14th 1950, G-AKVS had succumbed to peer pressure and in place of a nice but unpopular control wheel, had a conventional control column and rudder bar. Powered by a Cirrus Major 3, it proved to be the Chrislea company's last-ditch attempt to break into a light plane market dominated by Austers and Miles. As well as the usual features, the top deck of the rear fuselage was removable so a stretcher could be laid inside. Promoted as a light freighter or air ambulance, the Skyjeep was later offered with a 200 hp Gipsy Six in 1957. G-AKVS was sold to France in 1952 – the same year when Chrislea's assets were sold to C E Harper Aircraft Ltd of Exeter Airport. Chrislea faded from the game.

One of the saddest casualties of the Ministry of Transport & Civil Aviation's insistence on the correct paperwork as a top requirement for considering airworthiness, the Bücker Bü.181 Bestmann, G-AKAX, must come near the top of the list. This two-seater, single-engine fully aerobatic aircraft built by Bücker Flugzeugbau GmbH in Rangsdorf, near Berlin was extensively used by the Luftwaffe in the Second World War. Named after a term used to denote a member of the deck crew on fishing boats, the prototype made its first flight in February 1939 and went on to became the standard primary trainer for the Luftwaffe. Powered by an in-line 105 hp Hirth HM 500 A or B engine, it incorporated split flaps, dual controls and side-by-side seating. More than 4,000 examples were built. This example was captured at the end of the war, quickly evaluated by the Air Ministry and then allocated the civil registration G-AKAX on July 10th 1947. Transported to Denham, it was assembled ready for flight, the paperwork being thought but a formality. However, no 'authorisation to fly' ever materialised even though German log books and relevant paperwork were supplied. The almost new aircraft was picketed down outside the old blister hangar on the west side of Denham Aerodrome and there it stayed, quietly deteriorating. Once perfectly airworthy, this delightful machine was finally broken up where it stood in 1950.

Captured German aircraft ranged from the obvious types to the unusual and the unique. One of the machines brought back to Farnborough at the war's end was this all-wood monocoque Zaunkoenig, originally built by the students of Brunswick University and given the German civil registration D-YBAR. Once ensconced in Hampshire, it was allocated the British serial number VX190. A small single-seat experimental aircraft, it was originally intended to have wings and tailplane that pivoted about their chordlines, but this feature was not fitted to this example. Quickly declared surplus by the Royal Aircraft Establishment, it was thoughtfully passed to the Experimental Group of the Ultra Light Aircraft Association at Elstree where it was accorded the out-of-sequence registration G-ALUA.

The Zaunkoenig was a really practical ultra-light and it was superbly built with a plywood monocoque fuselage. This head-on view taken at Elstree in 1947 shows it standing on wheels and skid – but note how high the tailplane is. The stick-back attitude also shows how big and effective the elevators were. The high-lift wing meant that one was airborne at 28 mph and spot-landings were delightfully easy.

Thanks to its superbly-deigned flaps and leading-edge slots, the Zaunkoenig – German for 'Wren' – was an incredibly slow flyer. This ensured that it also had a very short take-off and landing run, some while before the acronym 'STOL' had become fashionable. The 51 hp inline inverted Zundapp engine was largely of magnesium and was both very small and extremely light. The only problem was that it was always hard work to start – and almost impossible when hot. Many of the Experimental Group members gained their daily exercise prop-swinging the thing. Here it is seen running up outside the ULAA's 'blister' hangar with its 'weather-proof' canvas doors at Elstree in 1951.

With the soubriquet of 'the oldest jet-plane in the world', the Miles Sparrowjet was a straightforward Miles M.5 Sparrowhawk first flown in August 1935 and redesigned at Redhill as a single-seater in 1952 where it was retrofitted as a pure jet powered by a Turboméca Palas in each wing root. Flown by Fred Dunkerley, it managed to top 228 mph, winning the 1957 King's Cup Race. Like other small jet-powered aircraft, it was problematic to start and seemed to require rather a lot of cumbersome ground equipment to get the turbine started. Once both engines were powered up, however, the problems were far from over because there was insufficient thrust to overcome the resistance of the small(ish) wheels on airfield-quality turf and this meant that two energetic heavyweights were needed on each wing-tip to provide brute force in getting the aircraft moving. But it was a good flyer. Unhappily it was destroyed in a hangar fire at RAF Upavon in July 1964.

Chairman of the Popular Flying Association, Harold Best-Devereux arrived at Elstree Aerodrome in a French Druine Turbulent and started a revolution! This proved to be the harbinger of French amateur aviation as far as we were concerned. Best-Devereux had one great advantage in that he spoke fluent French and this was largely responsible for his success in getting the French regulations, as far as home-building and Permit to Fly aircraft were concerned, approved in Britain. This small machine was the start of it all. Registered to Henri Gindre at Buc in December 1955, it spearheaded acceptance of the Turbulent in Britain and was the first non-British design to be approved for home-construction here. In this picture, Best-Devereux formates on one of Elstree's Austers for the camera of Charles Brown the ace aerial photographer. The author was pilot on this occasion. Many years on, in October 1995, F-PHFR, pictured here, was sold to Britain, becoming G-BWID.

Roger Druine's Turbulent, F-PHFR, which was flown from France to Elstree by Harold Best-Devereux as a precursor to getting the type approved for amateur construction in this country. The one-piece wing of the aircraft, complete with undercarriage, made it somewhat unwieldy to assemble unlike an aircraft with detachable wings where the wheels were integral with the fuselage or fixed centre-section. Assembling a Turbulent meant holding the wing steady while you lifted the fuselage into place.

Here is one of the first British-built Druine Turbulents, G-APWP, built in 1961 by Colin Frederick Rogers, an engineer with Handley Page Aircraft Ltd. The engine was a 40 hp Pollman HEPU – a 1,200 cc VW-derived four-cylinder powerplant. Later fitted with wheel spats and 'go-faster' cowlings, this aircraft attained a straight and level speed of 135 mph which is thought to be the fastest speed any Turbulent ever attained. This aircraft enjoyed a worthwhile life until it was withdrawn from use in 1970.

The Druine D.31 Turbulent was 'adopted' by industrialist and aviation enthusiast Norman Herbert Jones (1905-91) of Rollason Aircraft & Engines Ltd. Jones was also the leading light behind the celebrated Tiger Club based at Croydon and later Redhill Aerodrome. Norman Jones put the Turbulent into production, building something like 30 examples including one which was flown by HRH The Duke of Edinburgh. Most operated on a special category Certificate of Airworthiness: three had a full C of A. Almost all had 'trademark' out-of-sequence registrations that ended with the letter 'Z'. Here we see four Tiger Cub Turbulents performing a low formation fly-past at Rochester in 1979. On the ground is Cessna 402B G-BAWZ, Fuji FA.200-160 Aero Subaru G-BDFS and Piper PA.28 Cherokee 161 G-BGKR.

Air Commodore Christopher Paul's Druine Turbulent, suitably registered G-AJCP, was fitted with a sliding canopy. This registration had originally been reserved for an Avro Anson which was not converted at the war's end and was thus available when the worthy Air Commodore was doing his research. A Rollason-built Tiger Club Turbulent, G-APKZ can be seen in the background.

Through the enthusiasm and financial backing of Norman H Jones, owner of Rollason, the Druine D.31 Turbulent was put through the rigorous programme of requirements to qualify for a special category Certificate of Airworthiness. The machines built to this specification are referred to as Rollason Turbulents and, with the exception of the first which took a special registration for its owner G J C Paul (G-AJCP), all Rollason built examples had registrations that ended with the letter 'Z'. G-APIZ was no exception. This one, first flown on April 2nd 1958, was owned and operated by the Tiger Club but crashed at Wells House Farm, West Clandon, Surrey, on May 25th 1963. The remains were subsequently rebuilt and the aircraft is still registered.

Only one member of the Royal Family has ever flown a single-seat aircraft solo, if that is not stating the too obvious. It will come as no surprise to those who know him that it was HRH The Duke of Edinburgh who, in 1959, did a circuit in G-APNZ, a Rollason Turbulent. The following year his equerry, Sqdn Ldr John de Milt Severne (1925-2015) flew the same aircraft in the King's Cup Race – and won. Here the Royal tyre pressure is being checked. Note the Royal crest on the cockpit side.

Pictured at Redhill on January 14th 1962, this Druine D.31 Turbulent G-ARGZ was built by Rollasons of Croydon. It was one of several to be fitted with a neat sliding cockpit canopy and was operated by The Tiger Club, the logo of which appears directly below the cockpit entry point.

After Roger Druine's success with the little single-seat Turbulent he went on to devise a two-seat version which he called the Turbi. The first two of these to be made in Britain were built by students of the de Havilland Technical College at Hatfield (G-AOTK) and by the author for the Popular Flying Association via Britten-Norman at Bembridge (G-APFA). The type gained rapid acceptance in France where it was used for sport flying and training – something which was not allowed on a Permit to Fly aircraft in Britain. Here is the 46th example to have been built, F-WIYA, for the École de l'Air which is a military-based school training line officers in the French Air Force.

Of all the European countries it was probably France that was the first to restart amateur aircraft construction once the war was over. Indeed, there is some proof to suggest that a degree of home-building continued in France during the war, specifically after 1942 and in Vichy France, All this meant that once the hostilities were over, you might say that French homebuilders hit the skies running! One of the earliest designs available was the Jodel D-9, the design of Joly and Delmontez. Édouard Joly and his son-in-law Jean Délémontez formed a company in 1946 called Société des Avions Jodel at Dijon. Delemontez was a qualified aeronautical engineer, and Joly had built an aircraft before the war. F-PBXV was built at Beauvais in 1952 and flew into Britain where it attracted very great interest. By 1969 the first British-built examples were appearing and others were imported. Two-seat variants – the D-11 Club – followed. The one shown here, pictured at White Waltham, was written off at Beauvais in 1987.

This single-seat Jodel Bébé D-94, No.B-14, F-PDHQ, was constructed in 1950 by Robert Perdrix at Bourg. The view over the nose was exceptional even on the ground. Jodels, popular in Britain, were both pleasant and easy to fly while the elevators were not quite as sharp as those on the contemporary Turbulent by Roger Druine.

Although perhaps not quite as popular with British builders as the Turbulent, the Jodel series of small aircraft had its following. The range of designs available was quite extensive from the open cockpit single-seater through cabin two-seater like this one right up to the later cabin four-place touring aircraft. Here is a French-built example of the two-seat D-112 No.108, F-PGKQ, constructed in 1954 by Romanian-born Marcel Jurca who, having built this aircraft, went on to design and build the aircraft which made a name for him – the Tempéte.

The Jodel formula was to survive through many decades of development. Its success seems to have lain in the fact that it was scalable in a literal sense. From the small single-seat, it gradually grew bigger and bigger until the four-seater Ambassadeur. On the way up was the closed-cockpit D-112 and this one, which visited England in the 1960s and 1970s, was built in June 1953. Long-term resident at Besançon, F-PGTE had a Continental C.90 engine.

From the Jodel D-9 of 1946 the design was developed by Jean Délémontez in collaboration with Pierre Robin to the DR.1050 Ambassadeur. Built from 1958 to 1967 by Centre-Est Aeronautique (CEA), also known as Robin Aircraft, and by Société Aéronautique Normande (SAN), several versions appeared culminating in the DR.1050M1 model which had a swept fin and rudder. This one, G-BAMW, was a three-seater with a 100 hp Continental O-200 engine. Since the collapse of the original manufacturers in 1968, the aircraft has only been available as a set of plans. A popular design of which more than 600 are alleged to have been built in France, the all-wood tourer had a span of 28 feet 7 inches and a tare weight of 970 lbs. For a small aircraft it had quite a high wing-loading at 11.7 lbs/sq.ft and turned in a top speed of 137 mph with a stalling speed of 55 mph.

After the success of the Turbulent and the Turbi, Roger Druine produced his very last design, the two-seat side-by-side D.62 Condor which was later put into production by Rollasons at Croydon. G-ARHZ dates from December 13th 1960. This picture was taken the following summer at Redhill Aerodrome. This Condor had the misfortune to be broken in a heavy landing on September 4th 1994, at Damyn's Hall Airstrip near the old RAF base at Hornchurch in Essex. Happily it still flies after a successful rebuild. Designer Roger Druine was a modest young man of immense talent but was a sufferer from leukaemia which finally killed him in March 1958. He was only 37 years of age.

Roger Druine's progression from the open-cockpit single-seat Turbulent through tandem two-seat Turbi to side-by-side Condor was an exercise in simple design progression. Rollasons of Croydon put the aircraft into production and, having built a few, made some modifications to produce the D.62B Condor of which G-ATSK is an example. This was fitted with two-position flaps (fully up or fully down) and a fuselage four inches shorter than the original. A large number was built fitted with the 100 hp Continental O-200 engine. This example was operated by Fairoaks Aero Club from May 1966. It was written off in a fatal accident there on July 20th 1973 following an attempted full-flap take-off out of wind on a short runway.

The story of G-AKBC is long and unfortunate. Intended to be a candidate for the post-war light aircraft market, the four-seater all-wood Newbury AP.4 EoN was the product of furniture-makers Elliotts of Newbury. During the war this firm had been a prime supplier of aircraft for the war effort, but in 1946 when it applied to be allowed to return to its pre-war joinery business, the government of the day prohibited it, saying that the business was too important as an aircraft-builder and it might be needed again. The EoN was designed and built as a sort of 'default effort' by the firm to stay in business without contravening the covenant on its operations. The 100 hp Blackburn Cirrus Minor II-powered light blue and dark blue cabin aircraft was a delight to fly, making its first flight at Welford in Berkshire piloted by one-time Gloster chief test pilot Phillip J Stanbury (1921-79). The EoN was later upgraded with a 145 hp Gipsy Major 10 and given a longer nose-wheel leg but it was an expensive aeroplane, more costly than a new Taylorcraft Auster or a government surplus Tiger Moth or Magister. The EoN was popular wherever it went, but it did not sell. Eventually it was destroyed following a silly and totally avoidable pilotless take-off at Lympne on April 14th 1950. The era of the EoN was over.

The French are famed for taking unusual approaches to light aircraft design. Some work, others are not so good. However, one which taught aircraft designers a great deal was Albert Gatard's tiny single-seater of 1957 which he called the Statoplane. Spanning 21 feet and with a length of 14 feet 11 inches, this 24 hp VW-powered wooden wonder weighed just 375 lbs empty. Intended for home-building, this was visually characterised by having a huge cockpit bubble canopy which provided ample headroom for even the tallest pilot. Aerodynamically it had no elevators, the variable-incidence tailplane being provided with endplates. The method of climbing was unusual. Instead of adjusting the pitch of the wing by using the elevators to adjust the angle of attack of the wings, Gatard employed wing flaps while trimming the tailplane to balance out any change in pitch. This allowed the aircraft to achieve its maximum rate of climb while maintaining the fuselage within 4° of level. The additional aerodynamic drag caused by the lowered flaps was balanced by the drag saved by keeping the fuselage level. These flaps were therefore connected to the control-column. Here F-PHUO flies with Gatard at the controls. Unusually, the type did not catch on in Britain.

The Piper L.4 Cub was one of the nicest early post-war American aircraft. As a tandem two-seater with doors on the starboard side – as usual on US machines – it was a joy to fly. Many appeared on the British register and a large number still survive to be cherished by their owners. G-AKAA was once a resident at Elstree and later at Little Snoring where this picture was taken. First registered here on June 23rd 1947, as a L.4B, this version is distinguished over earlier variants by its aerodynamically-balanced rudder. At one time this flew with smart aerodynamic wheel spats.

G-AKDN was a Canadian-built de Havilland (Canada) DHC.1 Chipmunk, one of the initial two that were sent over to Boscombe Down for Service trials in November 1948. It was readily accepted into the realms of the RAF as a training aircraft to replace the antediluvian Tiger Moth. Finished in polished aluminium and green, it is pictured here in the 1950s when it was operated by The London Aeroplane Club whose insignia is visible on the cowling. The aircraft was later based at Knettishall, Suffolk.

Another view of G-AKDN in bucolic setting. British-built aircraft were subtly different from the Canadian-made examples. The undercarriage, for example, was slightly further forward. When the type became obsolete in RAF service, flying clubs bought up many only to find that the programme of conversion to civilian standards which was demanded by the Ministry of Civil Aviation was long and expensive. One of the earliest to be converted was Elstree Flying Club's G-AOSY – but it required many hours of work to get there.

Displaying its Class B markings for Slingsby Sailplanes, G-26-1 was the prototype T.29B Motor-Tutor powered by an Aeronca JAP J.99 37 hp flat twin air-cooled engine. This would later take the civil registration G-AKEY. It is pictured here on an early demonstration flight. In the background is Tony Cole's Comper Swift, G-ABUS.

When in the late 1930s, the Aeronautical Corporation of Great Britain at Peterborough went into receivership, its two associate companies, Lang Propellers Ltd and J A Prestwick Ltd, were able to step aside untainted. Prestwick had a large stock of its own improved variant of the Aeronca E.113C engine which, as the JAP J.99, had been fitted to British-built Aeronca 100 two-seaters the sales of which were handled by a distributor at Hanworth Aerodrome. This stock of JAP engines kick-started the home-built aircraft movement in the 1940s and 1950s. Slingsby Sailplanes had the idea of converting a two-seat Tutor glider into a single-seat powered aircraft with the intention of introducing a degree of self-training for the Private Pilot's Licence. The hope was that once a student had been cleared for solo flying he could complete some if not all of his subsequent hours (then standing at 40) to qualify for his Licence. The upshot was the Slingsby Motor-Tutor with conventional undercarriage and a brand new 37 hp air-cooled flat twin on the nose. Three were built – G-AKEY (later also flown as G-26-1) first flown in August 1947, G-AKJD of October 1947, and, later, G-AZSD in 1972.

The most popular Motor Tutor – the second built – was G-AKJD and Slingsby used this both as a demonstration model and as a vehicle for improvement. In this view of the aircraft notice the large, bulbous fairings under the wings which not only conceal the aileron operating cables but also provide a housing for aerodynamic mass-balances whish were added to avoid aileron flutter. While no cases of such a problem were known, Fred Slingsby must have had some reason for fearing the manifestation of such a characteristic. Meanwhile, Slingsby's grand plan for the Motor Tutor in 'part-solo flight training', despite being backed by the Popular Flying Association, was rejected out of hand by the licensing wallahs at the Ministry of Civil Aviation. The Motor Tutor was thus a solution to a problem that officially did not exist and so a great idea faded. G-AJKD was written off following a crash on Dunstable Downs on June 21st 1964. So ended a good idea.

One of the great 'white elephants' of the early post-war years was the Planet Satellite. Projected as all things to all men, this magnesium-alloy four-seater had a retractable undercarriage, a buried, mid-ship 250 hp Gipsy Queen 32 engine and a pusher propeller. Built in the old Redwing factory at Croydon, it was designed by J N D Heenan and a company was formed that comprised some very big industrial names. The impression was that the bigger the backing firm, the better the product. It wasn't. Static star of the first SBAC show to be held at Farnborough on 7th September 1948, G-ALOI was taken to Blackbushe for its first take-off trials. The 33 ft span wonderplane would not fly. Some simple aerodynamic calculations would later prove why. The earth bound Satellite was scrapped while a second fuselage was turned into a helicopter that was also a failure. The Planet Satellite is one of those non-flying wild-cards that gained immortality through spectacular and well-publicised failure.

While on the subject of failures it is worth mentioning another aircraft that, while it never got quite as far as the Planet Satellite, was a close runner. The Bellamy-Hilborne BH.1 Hampshire Halcyon was a tricycle-undercarriaged twin-engined four-seater that looked to have a great deal going for it. Designed by Ray Hilborne (seen standing at the right in this picture) and built under the auspices of the Hampshire Aero Club at Eastleigh under the sponsorship of Vivian Bellamy, the Halcyon was intended to be the cheapest twin with a selling price estimated, in 1959-60, to be 'under £5,000'. Registered G-ARIO on January 30th 1961, it had a monocoque fuselage built using cold-cured diagonally-wrapped plywood in a similar manner to the DH Mosquito. Power came from two four-cylinder in-line Walter Minor engines and later versions were proposed to take the Rover TP.60 gas turbine already air-tested in the Club's Currie Wot biplane. Construction was a slow process and finally taxi trials were ready to be undertaken. It was at this point that all went wrong. The engines were a long way in front of the main wheels which were attached to the rear spar. Moving over rough ground generated unexpected twisting forces that fractured the centre-section rear spar. It was February 17th 1962. The Halcyon was deemed damaged beyond repair for it was a fundamental design flaw. So ended a promising venture.

The early goal of the Ultra Light Aircraft Association, forerunner of the Popular Flying Association and now the Light Aircraft Association, was to have a British aircraft design for amateur construction. Other than the pre-war Luton LA.4 Minor, there was nothing. When two former de Havilland Technical College students, John Britten and Desmond Norman, announced that this was a brief they could meet, everybody in the top brass of the ULAA backed them, urging them forward. They even provided one of their brand new, pre-war surplus 37 hp Aeronca flat twin engines from a stock built up by manufacturers J A Prestwich at its London factory. The two young men rented space in the hangar then belonging to Bembridge Flying Club, and hired Pete Gattrell, a local aircraft carpenter, to work on the project with them. They called it the BN-1F or, in a reverse alliteration, 'Finibee'. Here is the fuselage of the first incarnation pictured on July 22nd 1950. Note the heavy steel cantilever undercarriage beam, each leg attached to the fuselage by fourteen ¼-inch diameter steel bolts.

The BN-1F incorporated many features, some controversial, others useful. The ULAA accepted all the two young men offered with open arms. These included a novel form of internal wing bracing where individual ribs only had vertical members and every other rib bay in the span was plywood-covered to provide stiffness. The whole wing trailing edge was hinged – two outer ailerons, one central landing flap with central 'pilot's head' cut-out. Here builder Pete Gattrell poses with his handiwork in July 1950. In due course, Desmond Norman, not always the best choice, despite his background on Vampires in the RAF, attempted the first flight. The high-drag aircraft proved woefully underpowered and directionally wayward. It drifted sideways into the ground and the undercarriage was ripped off, predictably breaking the fuselage at the cockpit. The BN-1F was an over-engineered and overweight aircraft and ought to have been abandoned there and then. Instead of this, a series of increasingly desperate modifications was made in an attempt to make it fly satisfactorily.

The first version of the BN-1F, registered G-ALZE, was not a success. The second one, which had an entirely new fuselage, was powered by a 55 hp Lycoming flat four and had a conventional braced undercarriage of tubular steel. A rather ugly dorsal fin preceded the grossly extended rudder. Each wing had its span increased by adding a pair of full-chord ribs outboard of the ailerons.

Here the BN-1F 'Finibee' – now being dubbed the 'Funnybee' – reveals details of its 'sensible' undercarriage which was lighter than the prototype and did not impose twisting stress loads on the fuselage lower longerons.

In this three-quarter rear view the extra wing span can be seen and also some detail of the central landing flap the use of which was never fully evaluated because the change in pitch was both sudden and sharp at the first movement. After trials still proved the aircraft directionally unstable, two 'Zulu-shield' additional fins (rather like on the DH.86B Express airliner of 1938) were fitted into the outer ribs of the tailplane. Even this barely solved the problem and the ULAA executive committee had to come to terms with the harsh reality that the BN-1F was a hotch-potch and, despite the add-ons and alterations, still not an ideal flyer. At this point, the author was invited to take the pre-war Luton LA.4 Minor design and revise it to bring it up to date. On the hangar's 'mezzanine shelf' in the right background just above the aircraft's fin can be seen all that was left of the fuselage of the original machine.

A somewhat rural scene in a field at Hillington, King's Lynn, back in 1966. Auster J-1N Alpha G-AIGM stands in the grass with a Hornet Moth, a Miles Messenger and Auster J-5G Autocar G-AOIY. *Picture by M G Sweet.*

The Auster J-5F Aiglet or 'short-span' Auster was popular as a trainer and probably the best-remembered model was Tom Hayhow's G-AMOS *Liege Lady*. In this machine he set up no fewer than 28 point-to-point records in the C(1B) international weight class. These flights all took place between Elstree, Denham and Fairoaks and the principal European capitals. On April 10th 1953, he set off from Denham on an attempt at the Belgrade record but never arrived. A desperate search of the Alps was undertaken but neither he nor the blue and yellow aircraft was found until a party of skiers discovered the inverted Auster on May 25th at 6,000 ft above sea level. A search of the empty cockpit suggested the pilot, 46-year-old Thomas William Hayhow, had been unhurt in the accident. His body was eventually found 600 yards away. Clearly he survived the impact but was not dressed for the conditions and probably expired from exposure as he attempted to escape. It was thought that bad weather had forced him to return to the safety of Salzburg when he hit terrain between the Grosse and Kleiner Breitstein peaks.

This Auster J-5G Autocar, G-AMZV, was involved in joint experiments carried out between Auster Aircraft Ltd and Cowes-based Saunders-Roe Ltd to see if it could be operated on water. Unlike a flying-boat or seaplane, however, the idea was to employ water-skis, land on water and then taxi ashore onto firm sand. Extensive experiments were carried out off Ryde on the Isle of Wight where shallow water extends some considerable distance from the shore. Here the Auster could land on water skis and then turn for the beach and taxi up the sand. The experiments began with flotation tanks under the wings 'just in case' but it was found to be so easy to handle on the water-skis that these were done away with early on in the trials. Two weights were added to the aft fuselage (below the letter 'G' of the registration) to reduce chances of a nose-over on touch-down. The trials were successful but nothing further was done. The aircraft was sold to Giro Aviation Ltd of Southport in 1960 where it was used for joy-riding, and then passed on to Mell-Air Ltd of Weston-super-Mare. It was here that it crashed on August 28th 1966 when engaged in low-level aerobatics. Trying to avoid HT cables it stalled and crashed inverted killing the pilot and three passengers including two children.

Pictured at Rhoose in 1970, Miles M.38 Messenger G-AKIR shows off its high-lift landing flaps. Interestingly, this self-same wing design was also used on the twin-engined Miles Gemini as were the trailing flaps. This particular aircraft crashed at Leverton Outgate, six miles north-east by east from Boston, Lincolnshire, on June 5th 1971.

Miles M.38 Messenger 2A G-AJFC was first registered in March 1948. In December 1966 it was sold to Ireland, becoming EI-ADT seen here parked on what appears to be a scrap-heap and next to an Auster that has lost a rudder and one elevator. In the centre, under a rain cover, is BA Swallow 2, EI-AFN, the former G-AFGV which went to Ireland in August 1950.

Here is a fine study of the prototype Tipsy Junior OO-TIT soon after it was built in Belgium by Avions Fairey at Gosselies. It was the first of only two to be constructed, the second being OO-ULA, now G-AMVP since 1952. With a wing span of 22 feet 6 inches, the Junior was a nice aircraft to fly, but its high-drag ailerons could cause the novice pilot problems on landing and dropping a wing on landing was always a risk. As regards construction, the Junior was of normal four-longeron layout but the fuselage comprised a truss that was shallow in depth while of full width. Formers and stringers thus extended above and below the truss – an unconventional arrangement.

Tipsy Aircraft at Gosselies was the Belgian arm of Fairey Aviation Co of Hayes, Middlesex. The Tipsy Junior appeared in Belgium at the Cinquantenaire in Brussels on July 20th 1947, and was at once recognised as a worthy addition to the designs of the great Ernest-Oscar Tips. There were two prototypes, each slightly different – OO-TIT with a Czech-made 62 hp Walter Mikron four-cylinder in-line engine, and OO-TOT which never carried these marks but, in deference to the classification of 'ultra light aeroplane' became OO-ULA. This had a 37 hp Aeronca JAP engine supplied by the Ultra Light Aircraft Association. Each aircraft had slightly different wing-tips. Both machines were brought to England where OO-ULA was re-engined with a Mikron and re-registered G-AMVP. This aircraft made history on July 24th 1957, when test pilot Peter Twiss (1921-2011) took off from Ford Naval Air Station and landed on the aircraft carrier HMS *Ark Royal*. Drawings for the Junior were made available but the availability of cheap Tiger Moths plus obstinate legislation dissuaded home construction at that time. Tips was, in any case, well advanced with the Nipper which was an instant success. This aeroplane took part in the *Daily Express* race at Shoreham piloted by Fairey test pilot John Matthews where it hit 125 mph and averaged 109.5 mph.

It is perhaps hard to believe that the Tiger Moth first saw the light of day back in the heady days of 1931. At home in the post-war skies of the late 20th century as back in the days of King George V, it has also presented those with an inventive mind with endless opportunities to experiment. These individual aircraft have run the gamut from crop-spraying conversions (including the famous Australian VH-BUM which had no fabric on the rear fuselage) to four-seat rebuilds like the Jackaroo. Commonest of all, though, have been the cockpit hood conversions. While standard by environmental needs in Canada with the DH.82C, these enclosures come more into the luxury category in Britain. Styled 'coupé tops' by some, these vary in style and execution. One of the smartest conversions was G-ANSA, registered on May 26th 1954, with a conversion by Personal Plane Services of White Waltham that included large wing-root fairings, an extended exhaust manifold and wheel spats. Pictured here at Whitchurch, Bristol, on June 11th 1955, it met its end in the River Mersey near Speke on March 30th 1958.

The concept of the four-seat Tiger Moth was not as outlandish as may at first be thought, for the DH.83 Fox Moth was actually a five-seater on the same horsepower as the DH.82a. Some eighteen Jackaroo conversions were undertaken at Thruxton and many of them did yeoman service with the Wiltshire School of Flying based there. Three began life as crop-sprayers with Britten-Norman Ltd but they were not particularly successful in this role. Unpopular with their pilots, they did not handle as well as the nimble original two-seaters and were slower in the roll mode which affected their manoeuvrability in this specific task. Here G-AOEX, the former military Tiger NM175, flies four on a local sortee. Registered on October 10th 1955 it was withdrawn from use in February 1968.

The Thruxton Jackaroo was a four-seat cabin conversion of the DH.82a Tiger Moth devised in the early 1950s by Sqn Ldr James Edward Doran-Webb, managing director of the Wiltshire School of Flying at Thruxton. The idea had first been dreamed up by Ronald Prizeman who had thought of a four-seat high-wing aircraft made with Tiger Moth parts but having a new fuselage. Doran-Webb's idea used standard Moth parts. The front side frames of the Tiger Moth fuselage were moved apart by 12½-in within which four seats were installed, the starboard pair being staggered slightly forward rather like in the Tipsy Trainer. The basic structure and rigging of wings, tail and rear fuselage were unaltered but it was necessary to increase the undercarriage track by designing a new W-shaped centre truss and a top-wing centre-section fuel-tank frame. Two prototypes were built at Thruxton in 1956; G-AOEX was finished as a standard four-seater with cabin and known as a Series 1. It was test flown by Lt-Cdr Pat Shea-Simonds on March 2nd 1957. The Series 2, G-AOEY pictured here, was conceived as a cargo carrier/cropduster. The cabin could be converted to carry a load of 5501b and a new low-profile superstructure neatly converted the Series 2 into a single-seater with open cockpit. The Jackaroo as made by Thruxton was a rather angular, clumsy conversion. Later Rollasons made a conversion of their own on G-APOV which was better realised. However, the whole Jackaroo project turned out to be something of a 'nine-day wonder' and eventually virtually all were returned to two-seat Tiger Moth standard.

De Havilland Tiger Moth N6847 was sold off as Air Ministry surplus and registered G-APAL on April 4th 1957. Two years later, in May 1959, it was rebuilt as a Thruxton Jackaroo retaining its Tiger Moth registration. It remained as a four-seater and was a regular with the Winkfield Flying Group at Blackbushe Airport where this picture was taken in 1963. Eventually, it was returned to DH.82a status in July 1984.

G-AMNC was built as an Auster J-5B Autocar and operated by the Bristol Aircraft Ltd at Filton in January of 1952. Later converted to a J-5P by the fitment of a 145 hp De Havilland Gipsy Major 10 Mk.1 engine, it was exported to New Zealand in September 1957 as ZK-BVl. Austers established a very early toehold in New Zealand with the setting up of a distributorship with Boon & Co Ltd of Wellington.

This example of the Taylor JT.1 Monoplane, G-EBEVS, won the Best Homebuilt prize at the Popular Flying Association's annual rally staged at Cranfield in 1979. Here it is flown by owner-builder David Hunter. This aircraft was later fitted with an overall bubble cockpit canopy.

Spanning just 22 feet 9 inches, the Somers-Kendall SK-1 was an all-wood jet-powered racer with a tandem-wheeled landing gear and small wing-mounted outrigger wheels. Power came from one 220 lb. static-thrust Turboméca Palas 1 turbojet. Created by Hugh Woodley Kendall and built for J N 'Nat' Somers, the aircraft was proposed as a candidate for the Royal Aero Club prize for the design of an aerobatic racing light aircraft. A tandem two-seater, it featured a laminar-flow wing having an aspect ratio of eight. The leading edge and tips were made of fibreglass. Each wing contained a fuel tank, the total capacity being 227 litres. Camber-changing flaps extended over the entire span and the only metal parts were the engine mounts, the landing gear and butterfly tail. The undercarriage front wheel was a Miles Gemini tail wheel, with a single main wheel. The side outriggers fully retracted into the wing. The butterfly tail was all-flying and smaller trailing edge flaps act doubled as servo trim tabs.

Here Hugh Kendall pilots the SK-1. He made the first flight on October 8th 1955. While it flew beautifully, it was rather hopeless on grass, full engine power and often human aid being needed to overcome grass-resistance when taxying. This had also been a problem with the Miles Sparrowjet, G-ADNL. Tentative plans for the Somers-Kendall production saw the erection of a new brick and steel hangar at Panshanger but these came to nothing following a mid-flight turbine failure early on in testing. And hoped-for interest by the RAF, to whom it was offered as a training aircraft, did not materialise.

Despite its problems of which ground handling, already mentioned, was only one, the Somers-Kendal SK.1 was an outstanding design superbly built. Despite its provenly-reliable French jet engine in this installation there were numerous minor problems that required time and money to sort out – both of which were in short supply. Another problem was that while the aircraft flew well it was a problem child on the ground, often there being insufficient thrust (or big enough wheels) to taxi back after landing. Once in the air, it was superb. On the ground, it invariably needed a person on each wing-tip to get moving.

Aside from the problems of developing 'real' aeroplanes, an interesting by-product of the post-war years was the creation of films dealing with early aviation. After the fiasco of the pre-war attempts in this realm – particular Alexander Korda's *The Conquest of the Air* – the new era of post-war movies was more venturesome. Remembering that Dart Aircraft had made replica aircraft for Korda, when Twentieth Century-Fox Productions Ltd decided to make a film called *Those Magnificent Men and their Flying Machines*, the producers decided to push the boat out and have replicas of not just one but a large number of early aircraft. All over the country, people were commissioned to build these replicas and so Bristol Boxkite, Santos-Dumont Demoiselle, Avro and others were soon appearing. It made for amusing work for a number of people. Harold Best-Devereaux and the author had the job of building the flying replica of the 'Eardley-Billing Biplane', seen here at Stapleford Tawney in the 1960s. The engine was a 65 hp Continental 'camouflaged' to look like a V-eight. We both managed to fly it.

The Piper Super Cub was an upgrade on the ordinary Piper J.3 Cub the history of which goes back to 1937. The example pictured here is registered as a model PA.18-135 or L.18C and was first operated by the American forces in Europe before being civilianised in Belgium as OO-GDG. It arrived in Britain and was registered G-BSHV on July 5th 1990. More recently it has succumbed to the heinous practice of undergoing a quite unnecessary change of registration as a variant of the motorist's 'cherished number-plate' craze. It is now G-GRIZ.

The original Piper L.4 Cub was rather unsophisticated but was such a joy to fly that it has earned the reputation for being the best thing that ever came out of America since the hot dog – assuming that you like hot dogs, that is. Pictured here is a Lycoming 65 hp-powered model L-4H – technically a Piper Grasshopper. Originally in France as F-BEGK, it came to England in December 1981 and took its fresh identity as G-BJTO. A feature of the type was the horizontally-split cockpit doors. Half opened downwards and the top half opened upwards and could be secured to the underside of the wing. The aircraft could be flown with these doors open – a delight in summertime skies.

The Percival P.40 Prentice was Percival Aircraft's 'troublesome child' and, like de Havilland's long drawn-out struggle with the DH.94 Moth Minor, it took an inordinately long time to iron out its aerodynamic quirks. The Prentice's problems were mostly elevator-sourced which is why the tailplane of the finished aircraft ended up such a strange shape. Anyway, the RAF used the aircraft as a trainer for a while but it was not a popular choice and came the day when they were replaced. Eagerly, Freddie Laker's Aviation Traders Ltd of Southend bought up 252 of them and enthusiastically created the biggest-ever single batch of civil aircraft registrations. Some 28 were converted between 1955 and 1958. Nobody wanted these large, cumbersome aircraft with their thirsty 250 hp Gipsy Queen 30-2 engines. The rest languished in a heap until eventually scrapped. One was actually turned into a seven-seater. Here we see G-AOKF which first flew as a civil aircraft on April 19th 1959 but was ultimately sold in Liberia.

Auster Aircraft eagerly grasped at every opportunity to expand the range and duties of its aircraft and when Bembridge-based Britten-Norman Ltd and its sister company Crop Culture (Aerial) Ltd began looking at the Rearsby Rooster as a potential crop-sprayer, the firm immediately laid down plans for a dedicated Auster Sprayer. The present author was despatched to Rearsby and worked with the company on the modification of a standard J-1 to agricultural standards. The result was the J-1U Workmaster of 1958 which was based on the Aiglet with an Autocrat fuselage, enlarged tail with dorsal fillet, large-diameter low-pressure tyres and a 180 hp Lycoming flat four engine. Britten-Norman rotary atomizers were mounted under the wings and a long 100-gallon chemical tank was placed in the fuselage next to the pilot with an extra seat behind for ferry-flying a passenger. A five-second dump-valve allowed emergency load-jettisoning while slotted ailerons and balanced elevators gave improved handling characteristics. G-APKP, the prototype pictured here, was registered on January 30th 1958 and subsequently operated in Nigeria where it crashed in October 1963. In all, Crop Culture operated nine Workmasters.

One aspect of amateur flight that developed surprisingly quickly with a wide number of adherents was the small autogyro. The post-war revival began in America with the creations of Igor Bensen and these inspired a number of UK inventors to take on and improve upon the concept. One of these who did more than most was Wing Commander Kenneth Horatio Wallis (1916-2013). A distinguished war veteran, he became a leading exponent of the UK small gyroplane earning 34 world records, eight of which he still held at the time of his death. His WA-116 Agile was the first of a range of ever-improving machines, one of which earned international fame in a James Bond film. G-ARRT was the prototype first flown on August 2nd 1961. Wallis Autogiros Ltd was eyed by Peter Masefield's Beagle Aircraft Ltd and 'invited' to join Austers and Miles to create a Beagle autogyro arm. Wisely, Wallis agreed but made certain he retained his company independence. Only five machines were built by Beagle, but Wallis was unharmed in the subsequent Beagle collapse. Wallis's development aircraft, seen here, was powered by a 72 hp Wallis-modified McCulloch 4318A flat-four engine.

A useful addition to Britain's post-war light plane portfolio was the Tipsy Nipper created by Ernest Oscar Tips of Fairey Aviation's Belgian arm, Tipsy Aircraft of Gosselies. The cockpit of this cantilever shoulder-wing aircraft was positioned between the wing spars providing a reasonably tight area that could not be extended. The view over the nose, however, was exceptional. Tipsy T.66 Nipper II, G-ARXN, was a Belgian-built example fitted with a HEPU engine.

This Tipsy Nipper Mk.II, G-ARBP, was Belgian-built, but later models were made in Britain first by Slingsby Sailplanes Ltd and later by Nipper Aircraft Ltd. What it lacked in attractive lines it made up for in utility for this small aircraft, powered by a derivative of the VW engine, proved both to handle well and be economical to fly. It was registered in June of 1960.

After an initial batch of Belgian-built Tipsy Nippers constructed by Avions Fairey between 1959 and 1961, the manufacturing licence was sold to Nipper Aircraft Ltd at Castle Donington and a new version called the Mk.III was manufactued for them by Slingsby Sailplanes Ltd at Kirkbymoorside in Yorkshire. Production was ended by the fire at Slingsby's in late 1968 which eventually led to the financial collapse of the business. The story didn't end there for Nipper Aircraft Ltd survived until May of 1971 when it ceased work and sold the licence to a company called Nipper Kits and Components, a company that serviced the amateur construction side of the market and supplied sets of drawings and components. Here is red and cream G-AVXD pictured when brand new in 1968. Described as a Slingsby T.66 Nipper, it lived on a private strip at Cupar in Fife. The Nipper had a welded steel tube uselage with a wooden wing and tailplane. With a weight of 364 lbs less engine, it is well within ultra-light limits. While early aircraft were fitted with the 40 hp Stamo VW variant, as pictured here, later examples were powered either by the 40 hp Pollman-Hepu or 45 hp Stark Stamo engines. More recently the 85 hp Jabiru 2200 engine has been successfully used.

G-AVKI was a Slingsby-built T.66 RA-45 Nipper Series 3 registered on April 24th 1967, and pictured here at Rhoose in 1977. The engine was a Sauer SE.1800 E.2S. This was one of a family of engines made in Germany by Sauer Flugmotorenbau of Ober-Olm. They were based on the Volkswagen engine, extensively modified for aircraft use. Certified for use in ultra-lights and powered gliders, it was widely used in aircraft such as the Nipper. With a fairly high compression ratio of 8.5 to 1, it produced a healthy 60 hp for a dry weight of 140 lbs. A novel aspect of the Tips-designed aircraft was the foot step to gain access to the cockpit. This was a narrow section of port wing root trailing edge, in the 'down' position in this picture, which could be lowered and was strong enough to take the weight of a kitted-out pilot. Nippers were prone to unintentional inversion if landed on rough ground, the nosewheel either digging in or collapsing. The high vertical centre of gravity did not help. G-AVKI did just that on October 17th 2017.

The summer of 1961 saw the arrival at Southampton's Eastleigh Airport of N22C, one of the four Cosmic Wind racers built in America by Toni LeVier and his associates. Named *Ballerina* and later registered G-ARUL, it was shipped to England by owner Milton Charles Blair and here Ron Benton and the author wheel it out of its hangar prior to some hair-raising flying. Blair also owned a Kensinger Midget Mustang, G-ASSV and this subsequently crashed with the owner at the controls killing him outright. Although it was established that he had been flying for many years and was a competent aviator, it was with some shock that the Inquest found that he had never held a licence! G-ARUL had its own fair share of problems, suffering a bad crash in 1966 from which it was restored. Span was 18 feet 11 ¼-ins and the all-up weight 840 lbs. With an 85 hp Continental C-85 up front, the Cosmic Wind's top speed was 185 mph. *Picture by Charles Everest.*

The formation of Beagle Aircraft Ltd brought forth several practical-looking designs, one of which was the single-engined all-metal B.121 Pup constructed by the company at Shoreham. The type made its first flight at Shoreham on April 8th 1967 as a two-seater. Soon a more powerful engine converted it to a three-seater and thence on to a four-seater. The Pup was a complex design to manufacture and was also corrosion-proofed throughout. Largely due to this, it was expensive to manufacture yet had to be marketed at a competitive price to match its mass-produced American counterparts. Besides this, it was a costly aircraft to maintain and one of Beagle Aircraft's weaknesses was that it tended to turn a blind eye to after-sales service and maintenance. Even Shoreham's own flying club had difficulty getting spare parts from the makers next door! While pilots liked the Pup, they had to accept the poor after-sales care. By the time government financial support for Beagle was withdrawn in December 1969 and the company went into receivership, more than 250 Pups were on order but production ceased with the 152nd aircraft. Some part-finished airframes were completed at a variety of locations. Here is G-AZCN, a Pup 150 registered in July 1971 and sold to Switzerland the following year as HB-NAY.

A slightly larger version of the Beagle Pup was the B.125 Bulldog, a two-seat side-by-side trainer which also had an optional third seat. The prototype first flew at Shoreham on May 19th 1969, and very quickly secured an order for 78 from the Swedish Air Board. However, the die was already cast and before any production aircraft could be built, Beagle was declared bust and ceased trading. Production rights, together with the order book, were taken over by Scottish Aviation Ltd at Prestwick and all the subsequent aircraft were built as Scottish Aviation Bulldogs. Later again Scottish Aviation would be absorbed by British Aerospace and the name of the Bulldog would change again. The largest home user was the Royal Air Force which ordered 130 machines in 1972. Here is G-ASAL, designated a Scottish Aviation Bulldog Series 120.

The British Executive & General Aviation Limited, better known as Beagle, was created in 1960 when the Pressed Steel Company absorbed the Auster Aircraft Company of Rearsby, Leicestershire, and F G Miles Limited of Shoreham, Sussex. Initially the purpose was to design the Beagle 206, originally a Bristol Aircraft idea. Heading up the operation was Peter G Masefield, former head of Bristol. Beagle turned out to be civil aviation's cause célèbre and its eventual financial collapse was almost an inevitability from day one. Initially the three parts of the company operated independently, the Rearsby factory as Beagle-Auster Ltd and the Shoreham factory as Beagle-Miles Ltd. This did not last long and the three parts of the company were merged as Beagle Aircraft Ltd in 1962. In 1965 parent company Pressed Steel was acquired by the British Motor Corp which, while not renowned for any experience in light aircraft design or production, requested government financial aid. The government responded by buying Beagle in 1966, but when more money was needed the company was put into receivership. Impossible to find a buyer in the trade, the firm was asset-stripped and sold off in 1969. The first aircraft to carry the Beagle name were developed from Auster designs. These were the Airedale, Terrier and D5/180 Husky. The Airedale and Terrier were intended as stop-gap designs to keep production shops busy and to be sold whilst more modern designs were developed. However, the firm lost almost £500,000 on the Airedale, due to its old design, poor performance and high cost while the Terrier was also unprofitable, due to the age of the design and the extensive amount of time it took to convert. The Beagle Husky was made in very small numbers and each was sold at a significant loss. In 1968, the Auster assets including all spares, jigs and partly completed airframes were sold to Hants and Sussex Aviation in order to make room for the production of the low-wing Pup. This made its first flight in 1967 and was sold in some quantity until the company's bankruptcy. The receiver disposed of a number of incomplete Pup aircraft which were then finished off by other companies. At the time of the company's bankruptcy in 1969, the military Bulldog was being developed from the Pup by Beagle. Here we see Beagle-Auster A.61 Terrier 2 G-ASAN of Peterborough & Spalding Gliding Club at Crowland Aerodrome. This Terrier was built from Auster AOP 6/T.7 VX928.

Known as the Piel CP.301a Emeraude, G-ASCZ was a fine example of a French home-built design. Claude Piel (1921-82) was born in Paris and went on to design two fine light aircraft, this one and another called the Diamant. Piel worked at one time with Boisavia and later teamed up with Robert Denize to design the CP.20 which marked his first use of an elliptical, Spitfire-like wing planform. This formed the basis of the Emeraude for which the two men created a business called Copavia. This did not last so Piel joined the Société des Constructions Aéronautiques du Nord (SCANOR) which also took over Emeraude production. In 1959 Piel moved to Scintex and the following year they developed an Emeraude variant, which had a sliding canopy instead of the upward-opening doors of the earlier model. Scintex also built the Super Emeraude, with an airframe strengthened for aerobatics and a cleaner external design. The majority of Scintex Emeraudes and Super Emeraudes were built at the Menavia factory at Clermont-Ferrand. Meanwhile Piel sold sets of plans for the aircraft to amateur builders. It was said to be a difficult aircraft to build due to its tapered box spar and inevitably that no two wing ribs were the same.

G-ASIB was an American Cessna, this one being a 172D Skyhawk, which first appeared on the British register in May of 1963. This all-metal, single-engined four-seater first flew in 1955 and is described as the most popular aircraft ever built, more having been produced than of any other aircraft. Defined by longevity and popularity, the 172 is the most successful aircraft in history. Cessna delivered the first production model in 1956 and by 2015 the company and its partners had built more than 44,000. The aircraft is still in production today. It began life as a tricycle landing gear variant of the tailwheel'd Cessna 170, with a basic level of standard equipment. In January 1955, Cessna flew an improved variant of the Cessna 170, a Continental O-300-A-powered Cessna 170C with larger elevators and a more angular fin. Although the variant was tested and certified, Cessna decided to modify it with a tricycle undercarriage, and the modified Cessna 170C flew again on June 12th 1955. Known as the 172, it became an overnight sales success, and over 1,400 were built in 1956, its first full year of production.

The many varieties of American Cessna light aircraft began to appear in our skies during the late 1950s, in the main European-built by the firm's agents, Reims Aviation. These aircraft all had a letter 'F' prefix, hence this model, G-ATBK, which is a 172F, is designated confusingly F.172F and appeared on the British register in March of 1965.

The Miles M.100 Student was a two-seat side-by-side private venture trainer designed by George Miles and test-flown as G-35-4 in September 1957. Later registered as G-APLK, it was powered by an 880 lb static-thrust Blackburn Turboméca Marboré 2A. Only one was ever built and, although successful, its development was beyond the financial resources of its maker. Sadly this fine-looking machine was another underfunded project candidate. It could have made a first rate trainer for the RAF had it been proceeded with.

The ancient pioneering French company Morane-Saulnier dates back to 1911 when Raymond Saulnier (1881–1964) and the Morane brothers, Léon (1885–1918) and Robert (1886–1968) joined forces to start an aircraft business. In post-war years, the business has undergone several changes of name and ownership as indeed has the entire aviation industry in France and in 1962 was acquired by Potez becoming the *Societe d'Exploitation des Etablissements Morane-Saulnier* or SEEMS for short. In 1966 its civilian models were disposed of to the *Societe de Construction d'Avions de Tourisme et d'Affaires* or SOCATA which is now owned by Aérospatiale. In the 1960s the firm produced the Rallye Commodore powered by a 145 hp Lycoming O-300-A. Imported into Britain by Air Touring Services of Biggin Hill, this aircraft and its variants enjoyed some popularity in the 1960s and here is G-ATST, a Rallye Commodore 180 introduced on April 4th 1966. *Picture by courtesy of M G Sweet.*

The 24-ft span Mitchell-Proctor Kittiwake I was a single-seat sports aircraft developed from the Mitchell-Prizeman Scamp design study created for the Rollason Midget Racer Competition of 1964. Winner of the third prize, this design was the work of Dr C G B Mitchell. Now with a variant to construct, the builder was Roy G Procter. The all-metal aircraft made its first flight on May 23rd,1967, and Mitchell-Procter Aircraft was formed to produce the Kittiwake prototype. However, some 17 months later the partnership was dissolved. Nevertheless, plans for home-builders were produced by Procter Aircraft Associates while Mitchell concentrated on the design of a two-seat development, the Mitchell Kittiwake II. G-ATXN had an all-up weight of 1,350 lbs which was heavy for a single-seater. The cruising speed was 122 mph and the range 490 miles.

The Mitchell-Proctor Kittiwake I could double as a glider tug. It was powered by a 100 hp Rolls-Royce Continental O-200-A engine. Meanwhile, designer Mitchell went ahead with a two-seat version called the Mitchell Kittiwake II.

Once American aircraft began to appear on the British Register in the 1960s, increasing numbers of Cessna and Piper products could be seen in our skies. This Piper PA-28 Cherokee was an all-metal four-seater produced in large quantities at Lockhaven, Pennsylvania, from 1961 onwards. Sales were handled in the UK by importers CSA Aviation Ltd of Kidlington, Oxford. With a wing span of 30 feet, these Lycoming-powered tourers could cruise at 130 mph with a 525-mile range. G-AVLE was registered on May 8th 1967.

Former test pilot David Lockspeiser (1928–2014) conceived what he called his Land Development Aircraft. This was a scheme for a low-cost, utility passenger and/or freight aircraft, the essence of which would be cheapness of operation in underdeveloped regions. To prove the concept, he designed and built a seven-tenths full-size aircraft known as the Lockspeiser LDA-01, G-AVOR. The engine was an 85 hp Continental C.85, but it was later refitted with a 160 hp Lycoming O-320. The LDA-01 was a single-seat tandem-wing monoplane featuring fabric-covered metal construction. The foreplane was the same design as the port and starboard wings of the main plane but of half the area. The intention was to reduce the number of spare parts needed by re-using the same wing component interchangeably in each location. All spare parts, except the main fuselage, could be carried inside the capacious rectangular body of the aircraft. The main wings were fitted at the rear-end of the box structure fuselage and the front wing was attached underneath the cockpit. Originally the fuselage had four wheels, one at each corner, allowing the aircraft to taxi over its freight load which could then be lifted up into the fuselage hold by an internal winch. The undercarriage was later changed to a conventional three-wheeler. First flown as Wisley on August 24th 1971, the aircraft was subsequently renamed Boxer 500 and re-registered G-UTIL. Plans were in hand to produce it at Old Sarum Airfield when vandals set fire to its hangar on January 16th 1987, and it was destroyed. Lack of finance prevented further development of this interesting project.

The first British-built GY-201 Minicab was G-AWEP built to drawings produced by Arthur Ord-Hume who acquired the rights to the aircraft in 1955. Constructed over 2,000 hours by Stanley Jackson, superintendent of the Process Division of BAC's Preston factory, it was first flown by BAC test pilot Roland Prosper 'Roly' Beamont (1920-2001) and subsequently won the Popular Flying Association's 'Best Homebuilt' contest in 1964. Beamont went on to buy the aircraft from Jackson and it is still flying today.

When the present author acquired the rights to the GY-201 Minicab in 1956, the first task was to produce a set of drawings to suit the British amateur aircraft constructor and to specify materials to UK requirements. The outcome was the Ord-Hume GY-201 Minicab and the first to be built to the British plans was G-AWEP by Stan Jackson. Here he is seen with BAE test pilot Roly Beamont in a good air-to-air snapshot.

After his success with the Bearn GY-20 Minicab and the Supercab, French aircraft designer Yves Gardan went on to design the Sipa (*Societe Industrielle pour l'Aeronautique*) series of two-seat touring and training aircraft of the late 1940s-1950s period. The prototype first flew on May 15th 1947, securing first place in a French government competition for light two-seat aircraft for aero club use. The first production S.90 was a low-wing aircraft with fixed tailwheel undercarriage and side-by-side seating for two. The engine was a 75 hp Mathis G4F. Just four examples were constructed. Then came a massive order from the French government for 100 aircraft for use by the aero clubs, and these were powered by the 75 hp Minie 4DC engine as the SIPA S.901. The first made its initial flight on June 25th 1948. Deliveries were completed in the early 1950s. Various other engines were later installed in the S.901. Here is a SIPA 903 which was fitted with a 90 hp Continental C90-14F engine. Formerly F-BGBY, this one was imported in June 1966. Unfortunately, having departed Netherthorpe Aerodrome on a local flight, it crashed into the Humber Estuary at Cleethorpes on August 20th 1967. *Picture by M G Sweet.*

G-BCLM is an original French-built Bearn GY-20 Minicab and was formerly F-BGSZ. Imported in 1974, it was fitted with a modified Jodel undercarriage. Unfortunately this crashed at Hurst Farm, Winchfield, Hampshire, on September 11th 1983, following a bad-weather take-off from a private air strip after which the aircraft spun in for reasons never determined.

France was very much a European leader in private and home-built aircraft in the immediate post-war years and it was the inspiration of the French that really enthused us here in Ancient Albion. Relaxed rules governing flying small aircraft allowed the design, evolution and production of a variety of aircraft that were effectively prohibited in this country. While France was not renowned for its legislative freedoms, the French as a race have a way with restrictive legislation that is refreshingly different. When through the single-handed labours of PFA Chairman Harold Best-Devereux did we get the Ministry of Aviation to accept rules and regulations based on the French system, we entered a new era of private flying and at the same time formed an aeronautical bond with the French that many seem to have forgotten today. Here is a two-seat SIPA S.901 monoplane built under a regime which we British did not tolerate – until the French helped us change it!

The Belgian business of Stampe et Vertongen began at Antwerp in 1923 when Jean Stampe and Maurice Vertongen got together to design and build small touring aeroplanes. Alfred Renard was the firm's chief designer and all early designs were prefixed RSV (for Renard, Stampe and Vertongen). By the early 1930s Alfred Renard had left to join a company he had formed back in 1925 with his brother Georges Renard as *Société Anonyme d'Avions et de Moteurs Renard*. The RSV company designation prefix henceforth changed to SV. The most successful design was the SV.4 of 1933, a tourer/trainer biplane powered by a de Havilland Gipsy III engine. The business was later renamed Stampe et Renard when Stampe merged with the Renard company. The SV.4 underwent many changes and improvements and was still being built in 1947. More than 50 were imported into Britain for the use of Norman Jones' Tiger Club at Croydon as well as the Rothman's Aerobatic Team and private pilots. *Picture by courtesy of M G Sweet.*

Popularly known as the Belgian Tiger Moth – and often confused with its Hatfield look-alike – the Belgian-designed two-seat Stampe et Vertongen SV.4 was a popular all-wood trainer/tourer biplane designed in 1933 by Georges Ivanov. It quickly became popular as an aerobatic machine and, not having the DH.82a's anti-spin strakes, could perform spins and rolls with greater ease than its British rival. The Antwerp-based firm built 35 examples before war shut the factory. Once the war was over, a successor company was formed called Stampe et Renard which built a further 65 aircraft between 1948 and 1955. These were used as trainers for the Belgian Air Force. A French aerobatic group, Pastrouille d'ñtampes, was formed which toured Europe giving displays. Based on the similarly-named French Air Force flight which, like our own Red Arrows, aerobatted in front-line aircraft, this group flew Stampes in death-defying formations. Here is a picture of a typical UK air show display.

The dual-control Piper PA.17 Vagabond was a side-by-side two-seater fitted with a 65 hp Lycoming O-145-B and was a product of Piper's Lock Haven factory in 1948. Three reached our shores in the late 1960s via France from whence they were imported by Doug Bianchi's Personal Plane Services Ltd of Booker. G-AWKD had completed almost two decades of service in France as F-BFMZ before flying in British markings after May 1968. It began its life as N4892H, becoming NC4892H. As of time of writing, this venerable Piper is still flying.

Post-event history has wrongly attributed the design of the Britten-Norman BN-3 Nymph all-metal four-seater to Desmond Norman (1929-2002). In fact the Nymph was almost wholly the design of John Britten (1928-77). Famously designed in 53 days under great secrecy and first flown by Desmond Norman on May 17th 1969, the sole example G-AXFB was intended to be assembled in under-developed countries which would build the aircraft under a technology transfer scheme. As an export-driven design, the Nymph was designed as a currency-earner for the nation. The engine was a 115 hp Lycoming O-235, but it was designed to take a variety of similarly-powered units. Unfortunately interest in the Nymph waned quickly and none were sold. After the company had been taken over by Fairey in 1972, Norman went his own way, taking the design of the BN-3 with him. Following the death of John Britten at the age of only 47, Norman unveiled the NAC-1 Freelance, which turned out to be a slightly-modified BN-3 Nymph with a new paint job and now registered G-NACA. This first flew on September 29th 1984. Despite the usual promotional activities, it didn't sell either. Here is the prototype Nymph on its press flight in May 1957.

G-AXFB, the Britten-Norman BN-3 Nymph 115 after it had been repainted. While the hype hyped, the clever Nymph did not sell and it was withdrawn from use on C of A expiry on May 27th 1970. Desmond Norman revived it, gave it another paint scheme and re-registered it G-NACI. It still didn't sell and so was eventually allowed to bow to the inevitable.

One of the smallest aircraft to have flown in Britain, albeit while 'short on the paperwork trail', the Ward Gnome had a span of 15 ft 9 ins and a length of 11 ft 6 inches. Built by a carpenter and joiner who was also a keen aeromodeller, Michael Ward of North Scarle, Lincolnshire, the all-wood G-AXEI had a 14 hp Douglas twin-cylinder horizontally-opposed engine dating from 1925. There is some confusion over the first flight and various claims that it was carried out by its designer, or Peter Anderson of Newark, or by Raymond Fixter and the place and date is equally uncertain although most sources put it as being at Wigsley in Lincolnshire on October 4th 1967. The wings, of Clark Y section, had a uniform taper from four feet at the root to three feet at the tip. Raymond A Fixter certainly bought the aircraft and made a version for himself. Only one Gnome was made and today this is in a Lincolnshire aircraft museum. It was said to cruise at 50 mph and to have a range of 50 miles. It never had any authorisation to fly.

Luton LA.4A Minor G-AXKH is a good example of how a well-built and finished home-built can look. Powered by a four-cylinder VW derivative engine, this handsome specimen of the popular post-war British design is complete with wheel spats and 'go-faster' paint job.

In 1937, Cinque Ports Flying Club chief engineer Joseph R Curry designed and built two single-seat biplanes, G-AFCD and G-AFDS. Each was slightly different and, oddly, they shared the same engine, an American-built E.113C out of an Aeronca C.3, so only one could fly at a time. These were practical, popular little planes and the designer called them the Wot 1 and Wot 2. Both were destroyed in 1940 during an air raid on Lympne. After the war, Currie became chief engineer for the Hampshire Aeroplane Club (HAC) at Eastleigh. Its chief instructor was Vivian Bellamy who got Currie to resurrect the pre-war design, as a result of which two more examples were constructed under the supervision of John O Isaacs. The first, registered G-APNT, made its maiden flight on September 11th 1958. G-APNT was then re-engined with a 62 hp Walter Mikron II and dubbed the Hot Wot; when later it was flown as a floatplane it was called the Wet Wot. A much later version would be trialled with a 60 hp Rover TP60/1 industrial gas turbine engine as the Jet Wot. Well-suited to home-construction, the first home-built example flew in 1963. Later design rights were sold to Dr John H B Urmston (trading as Botley Aircraft), who later passed the design to Phoenix Aircraft Limited. Here is Phoenix Currie Wot G-AXOL. The engine is a Mikron.

In 1938, Cecil Hugh Latimer-Needham designed the LA.4 Luton Minor ultra light. The present author revised the design, brought it up to post-war standards, incorporated two-piece wings and other refinements both aerodynamic and constructional. The outcome was the Phoenix Aircraft LA.4a Minor, the first British design to gain PFA approval after the war. In 1971, after Phoenix Aircraft had been liquidated, Group Captain Alfred Stanley Knowles decided to make a two-seat version by widening the fuselage and making other changes, including squared-off wings and tail. He called the result the Luton Duet and registered it as G-AYTT on March 4th 1971. It gained a special category C of A on June 24th 1974. He also referred to this as a Luton/Phoenix design, which it was not. The aircraft still flies as a Knowles Duet but is nothing to do with Luton Aircraft or Phoenix Aircraft. A second example was said to have been built by Colin Woods and registered G-DUET on December 19th 1978. This was deleted on April 30th 2002.

Eric C Clutton and Ernest W Sherry were the original designers of FRED (Flying Runabout Experimental Design) over a six-year period that ended with a first flight of prototype G-ASZY at Meir Airfield. Stoke-on-Trent, on November 3rd 1963. FRED was a single-seat all-wood parasol monoplane powered originally by a Triumph 5T motorcycle engine. Rather like the Slingsby Motor Tutor of fifteen years earlier, it was intended for the safe flight in the hands of novice pilots including reasonably experienced glider pilots. By 1968 it was flying with a converted VW engine. The 65 hp Continental A-65 has also been fitted. FRED had a 22 ft 6 in wing span, rendering the construction of the aircraft, with its two-piece wings attached to a centre-section, readily achievable in an average-sized garage or, as Clutton would say, dining-room. In mid-1967, Sherry left, his place as co-designer being taken by Albert Tabenor. Home-building plans were issued and some 30 to 40 examples made around the world. The high-lift wing gives it a slow but safe performance. Here is a good example of the type – G-RONW built in December 1968 by P Gronow and powered by a 1,800 cc VW engine.

The Clutton FRED remains a home-built classic as an aircraft designed for simple construction that was also readily dismountable and roadable – i.e. being capable of towing behind a small family car. Designer and builder Eric Clutton moved to America some years ago but took his original aeroplane with him and still flies his design in Yankee skies. All credit to him. This example, G-BBBW, was finished in all-over deep yellow with black registration. The engine was a 1,800 cc VW engine.

The American Piper company, renowned for its tandem two-seat Cub, also made larger machines such as this PA-31 Turbo Navajo aimed originally at small-scale cargo and feeder liner operators and the corporate market. As a light executive and utility transport it was a success making its first flight on September 30th 1964. Vickers Aircraft acquired this one in 1968 as a VIP transport. G-AWOW was registered on August 21st that year. Originally N9172Y, it was sold on to Denmark in 1975 where it became OY-DLY. With a 247 mph cruising speed from its two 310 hp Lycoming T10 turbocharged engines, it was no slouch.

The tiny all-metal Moni was the work of an American schoolteacher named John Monnett who deigned his sport aircraft in the early 1980s aiming it at home-builders. Essentially a single-seat low-wing motor-glider with a butterfly tail, it could be built with a single fixed mainwheel, a steerable tailwheel undercarriage, or a full tricycle. Power was provided by a 30 hp twin-cylinder horizontally-opposed air-cooled motor. With a length of 14 ft 8 in, a span of 27 ft 6 in and just 75 sq.ft of wing area, the Moni stands a mere 3 ft 6 in high. All-up weight is 500 lbs and the top speed of 110 mph is matched by a range of 320 miles. Here members look on in curiosity at one which arrived at an air display in Britain in 1998.

By the 1970s, Britain had adopted air-racing and this inspired W S 'Bill' Bowker of Farm Aviation at Rush Green to undertake construction of a US-designed OR65-2 Owl Racer. Designed by St Louis-born George Allen Owl (1920-81), the little all-metal Racer had a wing span of just 16 feet. Several had been built before and this one, G-AYMS named *Ricochet*, was air-tested by the legendary Sqdn Ldr Manx A Kelly (1932-76) on April 13th 1971. Unfortunately a defective, cut-down metal airscrew had been fitted and, after a day's racing at North Weald on May 31st that year, while on a positioning flight to Redhill, a blade disintegrated, the sudden out-of-balance load pulling the engine out of the airframe. Engine and prop remains fell through the roof of a Thamesside factory while the white and blue Owl crashed into the Thames at Greenwich Reach killing pilot and Formula One racer P T 'Terry' Gent-Eggett.

The Royal Aero Club staged a light aircraft design competition in 1953 and outright winner was the Airtourer, designed by Henry Millicer, chief aerodynamicist for Australia's Government Aircraft Factories. A prototype was constructed by a team in the Australian Ultra Light Aircraft Association at Williamstown, Melbourne, and registered VH-FMM in the late 1950s. It was first flown on March 31st 1959, by Flt Lt Randell Green at Moorabbin. This aircraft was demonstrated to clubs and schools as a possible replacement for the ageing Tiger Moths and Chipmunks. Development continued to an all-metal version, the first of which, VH-MVA, flew on December 12th 1961. Sydney-based lawn-mower and two-stroke engine maker Victa Ltd took over the project and both 100 hp and 115 hp-powered models were produced until 1966. Victa now sought Australian Government aid regarding tariff protection but this was not forthcoming so having made 168 aircraft, Victa shut down its aircraft division in February 1966. Manufacturing rights were sold the following year to Aero Engine Services Ltd (AESL) in New Zealand where further production of 115 hp and 150 hp models took place until 1973. Millicer had also designed a four-seater derivative design, the Victa Aircruiser powered by a 210 hp Continental O-360 engine, which was certificated in 1967. AESL acquired the rights to this in 1970 and it was used to form the basis of the CT/4 Airtrainer. Some 168 were completed by Victa in Sydney and a further 80 built by AESL in Hamilton NZ. AESL supplied fourteen kits of parts to Glos-Air Ltd of Staverton Airport, Cheltenham for completion and re-sale. Of these, Airtourer T.4, G-AZBE was registered in July of 1971. An aircraft which enjoyed world wide if short-lived, popularity, it was dogged by production and management problems. Some said it was underpowered: others found the centrally-fitted control-column uncomfortable, especially during aerobatics.

One of the Victa-supplied kits of Airtourer parts ended up as G-AZBE seen here at Staverton in the summer of 1971. This was shipped over on the SS *Delphic* along with G-AYWM in July 1969 and first flown at Staverton on July 19th that year. It flew with Lands End Aero Club and is still airworthy.

The Edgley EA-7 Optica was intended as a low-speed aerial observation machine for conducting some of the duties hitherto undertaken by helicopters. With this in mind, the designer, a retired school teacher and former chairman of the RAeS General Aviation Group named John Edgley, specified the aircraft as having a 'loiter' speed of 81 mph with a stalling speed of 67 mph. But it was in the aerodynamics and mechanics of the Optica that much virgin ground was cut. Optica had no fuselage and was powered by a 260hp Lycoming engine driving a five-bladed ducted fan buried in the rear fuselage which gave a very quiet cockpit. A free-suspended transparent pod housed the three-strong crew and gave almost unlimited 270deg visibility for pilot and the two passengers. Design began in 1974 by Edgley Aircraft Limited, formed by John Edgley and a small team at Old Sarum Airfield in Wiltshire which went on to build the prototype G-BGMW. The first flight took place on December 14th 1979. Able to stay aloft for up to eight hours, Edgley got the police interested for a surveillance role. The project received a sharp setback when a police demonstrator, G-KATY crashed on May 15th 1985, killing its crew of two. It was said that because the transparent nose gave no immediate visual horizon it was easy to stall. This assertion may be fatuous but some pilots found it disorientating to fly. Some 22 were built, but management and production problems and then receivership beset the project. There have been several attempts to re-start the project right into the present day.

A good view of John Edgley's Optica. Originally carrying the prototype marks G-56-001, it is seen with its subsequent registration as G-BGMW first flown on September 11th 1979. A British amateur design, it was aimed at part of the commercial market at that time undertaken by helicopters but a mixture of under-finance and sheer bad luck scuppered the project.

Edgley's demonstration Optina, G-BOPO reveals its peculiar shape as directed by the fact that it is powered by a ducted fan driven by a 160hp Avco Lycoming O-320 engine. This would later be upgraded to a 200hp IO-360. The engine drove a five-bladed fixed-pitch fan, and the Optica was promoted as the world's quietest powered aircraft. Edgley was a post-graduate student at the Imperial College of Science & Technology in London and began his design in 1974. A model was wind tunnel tested in 1975. Construction of a prototype began in London during 1976 and final assembly was undertaken at the College of Aeronautics, Cranfield, the first flight taking place on December 14th 1979.

The Edgley Optica showing its unconventional proportions. The ducted fan provided good sound insulation so the aircraft was very quiet in flight.

De Havilland Aircraft in Canada made a number of very successful light transport aircraft which saw service all over the world. These ranged from the Beaver and Otter to this, the Twin Otter which was a rival to the Britten-Norman Islander for small airlines and air taxi operators. Here is an interesting photograph showing one making what has to be the bee's knees of a spot-landing in a short landing demonstration. The aircraft was CF-SUL-X, a pre-production machine used as a company demonstrator in 1965 and a visiting attraction at our Farnborough Air Show.

Leavesden Aerodrome near Abbotts Langley in Hertfordshire had a rich history but in post-war years became the headquarters of de Havilland's engine factory, a relation of the original Stag Lane premises. When DH Engines was taken over by Rolls-Royce, many workers still remained loyal to the memory of Geoffrey de Havilland (1882-1966), a true aviation pioneer. In a poignant gesture, six workers marked the 100th anniversary of his birth by raising the flag of the old company at Leavesden. It was Tuesday, July 27th 1982. Six men remembered their old boss – from left to right, Terry Turley, Bruce Bosher, Peter Bryant, Gordon McLoughlan, John Williams, and Doug Valentine. Who says nostalgia's dead! Leavesden was finally abandoned by Rolls-Royce and the site became a film studio.

The agreement by which the Ministry of Transport & Civil Aviation undertook to accept the Certificates of Airworthiness issued by certain overseas countries, particularly France and Germany, removed a hurdle that had existed since the end of the war at which time importing foreign-built aircraft involved a copious amount of design investigation and almost as much paperwork as designed and building a new aircraft from scratch. Now private owners could buy an aircraft overseas safe in the knowledge that its authorisation to fly in its country of origin would be accepted by our authorities. Since France had spearheaded post-war light plane development, not surprisingly many such imports were Gallic in origin. Designer René Fournier built his first powered glider or motor-glider and fitted it with a VW engine. He then made an improved version with a Rectimo AR.1200 engine which met with great interest. Fournier formed a company called Societé Alpavia to produce a variant of the RF-2, the RF-3, which was exhibited at the June 1963 Paris Air Show. Series production began shortly afterwards. A number appeared in our skies, this one having been F-BMDD arriving in February 1975 as G-BCWK.

As the 20th century moved on, British owners were far more enterprising in what they wanted to fly and could afford to import. Sea-containers, unheard of back in the immediate post-war years, allowed cheaper sea freight costs and the standardisation of container sizes plus the introduction of special ships to carry them, brought world wide transportation costs down dramatically. One could now pack an aeroplane into a shipping container and send it half way round the world for an affordable sum. This was supplemented by a reduction in air-freight charges as transport aircraft grew larger. Many US-built aircraft began to appear on our shores, one being this Boeing Stearman A.75-N1 Kaydet, originally N51132 and, after June 1981, G-BIXN. On April 21st 1996, it crashed while flying from a small strip at Frensham Ponds, Farnham, and was 'destroyed'. It is reported that the aircraft is risen from the dead and is on 'protracted rebuild'.

Back in the days when things were less strict, you might find the odd home-built sitting at a commercial airport. Even, once in a while, a foreign-built one! This picture, believe it or not, was taken in the General Aviation park at Gatwick in 1986 and shows a Rutan Longez No.2113, F-PDEB which was on a visit from its base in Rouen. Visible over the starboard wing is a Piper PA.31 Navajo Chieftan 350 registered G-IFTA.

This Piper L-4H-Cub, G-BBXS was at one time N9865F. It is seen here powered by a Rolls-Royce Continental engine in a rather wintry setting amidst leafless trees.

William 'Bill' Bowker had been chief engineer for Agricultural Aviation Company Ltd at Panshanger in the 1950s but when that business closed he formed his own crop-dusting business at Rush Green using a variety of aircraft, Here is G-BEIJ, an American Schweizer Grumman Ag-Cat, originally N48685 and which he imported and registered on November 16th 1976. Developed from the Boeing Stearman formula, the Ag-Cat had a robust performance that centred on both solid and liquid chemical dispersal.

When designer Noel Pemberton-Billing proposed in his book *The Aeroplane of Tomorrow* (Hale, *c.*1941) that the aeroplane of the future would have a higher wing-loading, he wrote at a time when a light plane wing-loading of 7 lbs/sq.ft was felt to be at the top end of a perceived ideal world. In the early 1970s, French aeronautical engineer Michel Colomban (born 1932) designed what is still the world's smallest twin-engined single-seat aircraft – the Cri-Cri named after the sound of the cicada. With a span of just over 16 feet, the wing area of 33 sq.feet gives a wing-loading of 11 lbs.sq/ft. The tiny fuselage was dominated by a massive bubble canopy while the cantilever wing mounts the main wheels of the tricycle undercarriage. Two small petrol engines were mounted on pylons either side of the nose, each of these being a 15 hp single-cylinder JPX PUL 212 driving a small two-bladed wooden propeller. The whole aircraft was made from aluminum sheet glued to Klegecell foam. The aircraft was stressed for aerobatics and could fly satisfactorily on one engine. Top speed was 137 mph, range 288 miles and cruising speed 115 mph. Sold as plans for home-construction, builders have modified the design while one group demonstrated an electrically-powered Cri-Cri at the Green Aviation Show in Le Bourget in June 2010. Britttany Ferries used the Cri-Cri for promotional work and here is F-PYIJ pictured at Old Warden in 1989.

The star in the ascendant, in the opinion of many, emerged from Australia at the start of the new millennium with the attractive two-seater composite-constructed Jabiru light plane. Jabiru Aircraft Pty Ltd was set up at Bundaberg in Queensland by Rodney Stiff and Phil Ainsworth in 1988 to manufacture affordable light aircraft in both kit and finished forms. The first aircraft was certified by the Australian Civil Aviation Authority in October 1991. The range includes two and four-seaters largely built of composite materials to produce a strong but light structure with, in the main, tricycle undercarriages. The dual control system used a centrally-mounted control column. Originally fitted with an Italian-made aircraft engine production of which was discontinued, the Jabiru business scored when it began making its own four-cylinder engines, largely machined from the solid. By 1995 the firm was able to offer the Jabiru 2200, a horizontally-opposed four-cylinder air-cooled motor. From this was evolved the larger six-cylinder 3300 and eight-cylinder 5100 engines. Pictured at the Light Aircraft Association's Fly-In at Sywell in 2008, G-OJAB was originally a demonstration aircraft before being sold to a private owner at Elstree.

Microlight aircraft have come a long way since their beginnings back in the days of powered hang-gliders with Rogallo-style cloth wings. As aircraft in this category have become more and more like conventional aircraft, the microlight world has gained in impetus. The Kolb Twinster, pictured here, first flew in America in 1982 and now there are several flying in British skies. This practical-looking aeroplane incorporates a number of sophisticated features not the least of which is large landing flaps. The wings are described as 'quick-folding' and the empty weight just 450 lbs. Maximum speed with a 64 hp Rotax twin-cylinder two-stroke engine is 85 mph and the range a healthy 130 miles.

Desmond Norman's interesting take on mid-Atlantic style was his Freelance, a fresh makeover of the BN-3 Nymph which was designed by John Britten with some input from Norman. Britten was the talented designer for the company and Desmond the facilitator and sales guru. His claim to have designed the Freelance is a little wide of the mark since his modifications were not structurally fundamental, but, like Edgar Percival before him, Norman got the best designers to work for him and it was they that produced the designs for which Norman coined 'macho' names such as Fieldmaster, Firecracker and this one, Freelance. Resplendent with its go-faster wheel spats, G-NACI, the revised G-AXFD Nymph, made its first post-modification flights on September 29th 1984. Parts, including fuselages, for half a dozen aircraft were laid down but after Norman' s re-named company Norman Aircraft Company (NAC) failed to get a vital military order for the NDN Firecracker military trainer, the firm shut up shop. The unexpected death of Desmond Norman (1929-2002) while still actively engaged in seeking to promote his aircraft, marked finis to a determined man with a vision and his products. This picture shows the 'prototype' Freelance. A second aircraft was later completed and this was registered – again out of sequence – as G-NACA.

More of a utility aircraft was the NDN Fieldmaster, G-NRDC, a turboprop powered single-engined monoplane intended for agricultural duties. It was built in small numbers and used both as a cropsprayer and a firefighting aircraft. NDN Aircraft was set up in 1976 by Desmond Norman, one of the founders of Britten-Norman Ltd at Bembridge with John Britten, the manufacturers of the Islander. Originally intended to produce another of his designs, a trainer called the Firecracker, the firm now concentrated its efforts on the so-called NDN-6 Fieldmaster. This was a large single-engined low-winged monoplane with a fixed tricycle undercarriage, powered by a Pratt & Whitney PT6 turboprop engine. It was also the first Western-built agricultural aircraft designed for turboprop power. Unusual design features included an integral chemical hopper made of titanium and the integration of spray nozzles built into the flaps beneath the wings. The first prototype flew on December 17th 1981 at Sandown, Isle of Wight. The firm then moved the premises to Cardiff, South Wales, in 1985, renaming itself the Norman Aeroplane Company (NAC). Production finally started in 1987 but the firm went into receivership in 1988 after the production of just six Fieldmasters. Attempts to revive the project by Brooklands Aerospace were unsuccessful. Nigel Desmond Norman was involved in a number of design projects which resulted in several prototype aircraft of various designs. He died of a heart attack at Basingstoke railway station in November 2002 aged 73 years.

Desmond Norman, former partner in Britten-Norman Ltd of Bembridge, Isle of Wight, set up NDN Aircraft in 1976 with the goal of designing and building a piston-engined trainer designed to replicate the handling of a jet trainer. The outcome was the NDN-1 Firecracker of 1977. One associated target was that the aircraft would have a simple structure to allow it to be built under licence by third-world countries to help start up local aviation industries. The prototype, powered by a Lycoming O-540, flew on May 26th 1977. After the piston-engined prototype, NDN developed the aircraft by fitting a Pratt & Whitney Canada PT6 turboprop engine, producing the NDN-1T Turbo-Firecracker. Three NDN-1Ts were built for the British commercial flying school, Specialist Flying Training, which used them for contract training of foreign military students, the first flying in September 1983. The Firecracker was entered into the competition to replace the Jet Provosts used by the RAF as a basic trainer. Had it been successful, it would most probably have been produced by the Hunting Group but, although short-listed, it lost out to the Short Tucano. While NDN, in 1985 renamed the Norman Aircraft Company (NAC), continued to promote the Firecracker, no further interest emerged, and NAC went into receivership in 1988. Here NDN-1 prototype G-NDNI is seen in the air.